Traveling Towards Daylight

6/9/19

For Lisa

& poetry

[signature]

Designed and typeset by Sheep Meadow Press
Distributed by Syracuse University Press

Cover image: J.M.W. Turner: The Passage of the Gothard

Library of Congress Cataloging-in-Publications Data

Names: Marcus, Peter, 1958- author.
Title: Traveling towards daylight : new and selected poems / Peter Marcus.
Description: Rhinebeck, NY : Sheep Meadow Press, [2019]
Identifiers: LCCN 2019012202 | ISBN 9781937679859 (pbk.)
Classification: LCC PS3613.A7383 A6 2019 | DDC 811/.6--dc23
LC record available at: https://lccn.loc.gov/2019012202

All inquiries and permission requests should be addressed to the publisher.

The Sheep Meadow Press
P.O. Box 84
Rhinebeck, NY 12514

TRAVELING TOWARDS DAYLIGHT

NEW AND SELECTED POEMS

PETER MARCUS

Sheep Meadow Press
Rhinebeck, NY

Have I not forgotten at times who I am and where?
I come from another country. This is obviously why.
I remember, though, that even when I lived in the country of
my childhood I used to have the feeling that I came from elsewhere...
Not knowing where you come from is almost tantamount to admitting
that you come from nowhere.
—Edmond Jabes

If you set out on a journey pray that the road is long
a wandering without apparent aim a blind groping
so you come to know the earth's harshness not just but sight but by touch
so that you measure yourself against the world with your whole skin

...know the taste of water and fire of air and earth
for they will remain when all has passed away
and the journey remains though no longer yours
Then your homeland will seem too small for you
—Zbigniew Herbert

ACKNOWLEDGEMENTS:

Some of the poems appearing in this collection have been featured by the following reviews and presses: Ägni, The Antioch Review, The Bellevue Literary Review, Boulevard, Brilliant Corners, Caesura, The Café Review, Caliban, Cape Rock, Climate of Opinion, Confrontation, Connecticut Review, Crab Orchard Review, Cream City Review, Descant, Dunes Review, Gastronomica, Global City Review, Green Mountains Review, Harvard Review, Iowa Review, Kestrel, Landscape & Imagination, Little Pauxtene Review, Lost Horse Press, Miramar, The Missing Slate, Mount Hope, Mudfish, Mudlark, Negative Capability, New England Review, Nimrod, Noon, North American Review, North Dakota Review, Notre Dame Review, Pivot, Ploughshares, Poetry, Poetry East, Poetry International, Prairie Schooner, The Quarterly, Quarterly West, Rattle, Shabda Press, Shenandoah, Solo The Southern Review, Southwest Review, Spillway, Upstreet, Willow Springs, Witness, and Yellows Silk.

CONTENTS

TRAVELING TOWARDS DAYLIGHT

IN HUMAN RIVERS

THE NORTHERN HOURS

II. SMALL MYTHOLOGIES

III. SHORELINES

IV. THE SCALDING AND THE SCARING

IV. BORDERS AND CROSSINGS

I

SHATTERED SKIES
AND
THE SORROWS OF WATER

…the story…that remains somewhere between what I can't say and what I don't know.
—Pico Iyer

The best thing one can be is a horizon.
—Adonis

TORN PAGES FROM A GROUND ZERO NOTEBOOK

One body a moment ago that was a *person*
in a free-fall, *free*
as in the discount dying is at breakneck speed.

Though I was in the habit of saying to myself,
he jumped—

"Jumped," yes, but nothing like
"the jump" in jumping-rope
or going a little way up into the air to grab a rebound
or by pretending on Halloween that one is Superman.

No, definitely not *jumping,*
when all one had to do was climb out   on a ledge

and take a single

                    step.

One hundred stories up, their figures looked diminutive:
stockbrokers, bond-traders, dealers in insurance, prep cooks from *Windows*
of the World dicing celery and carrots. Men, women in kitchen aprons
and impeccably tailored suits, poufy chefs' hats like small inflated airbags.

Pizza box, briefcase, Apple laptop and actual apples, blue and white
Acropolis coffee cups, abandoned bicycles chained at the bases
of parking meters. Though mostly there are chains chaining
nothing.

I'm accosted by the faces alluded to as *missing*
on Plexiglas bus shelters, hospital facades, firehouse bricks.

Missing only as in being *missed*—
the Faces of *Love's Most Wanted.*

Faces marking life's occasions: at weddings, on fishing trips, on honey-
moons, at graduations, playing golf, riding horseback,

tanning in warm sand with a cooler-chilled beer,
skin aglow in coconut oil, (though I'd rather not ponder
the role of petroleum in all of this).
Muslim shopkeepers tape American flags to their storefront windows.
Terrified Sikh cabbies hide their turbans beneath their beds in Jackson Heights.
Each life brought to concision with narrative detail:
scars, birthmarks, dentures.

One wife writes
she's searching for
her husband who worked
on the 84th floor.
He has one glass eye.
Blue, she typed. *Blue.*

Beyond obstructing death, what else would I ask for?
A few weeks more without incessantly honking horns,
a permanent civility, fewer Americans obsessed
by the fate of contestants on *Survivor.*

The mayor pleads resume your "normal" lives,
watch baseball in the Bronx or Queens. Witness
a September *leaping catch* as an antithesis.

Glass eye, gold tooth, a set of false teeth
buried in the wreckage like the miniature jaw of a mastodon.

White columns of an Acropolis cup littered among the modern ruins.
Pizza box top mostly disintegrated except for the word *HOT* intact
with red serrated Armageddon flames.

As Lorca walked the Manhattan night
each nocturnal window reminded him of a tombstone.
Row upon row of tombstones stacked to the sky.

Among their obliterated tattoos:
a dragon that immolated its proprietor's body,
strangulation by anaconda,
death-dance to the rattle of the rattler,

inaudible music raised by the flute-loving python
until the owner is stupefied by poison.
Those with no notion of how their tattoos would transport them
aloft on quivering Monarch wings,
undulant on the lustrous hump of a porpoise.

In late October I notice signs of progress:
Kindergarten boys on a downtown playground,
not falling, not crying for their nannies or mothers,
but crashing toy airplanes into each other's bodies.
Is blinking passive or active?
Do our eyelashes fall or *jump*

or merely *flutter like living moths, like fire-*
blown ashes?

In March '01 the towering twin Bamiyan Buddha
blasted into rubble.

Taliban performance art?
I watch it over and over on YouTube.

A GREAT LIGHT OVER MORICHES, LONG ISLAND
THAT WAS FLIGHT 800

Twirling oak leaves, dead mosquitoes, drowning bees. The surface dance
Rearranges—choreography of disassembled wings. Contained motion,

water, breath, water, breath—the swimmer is a whirly-gig, approaching,
touching, pushing-off in azure wall-to-wall. *Tone the body and the brain,*

use good judgment and good taste. A few more laps then Blue Points with ale,
sunset through the pines in the Adirondack chair. In time as in water,

refreshment vanishes, fingertips wrinkled as prunes, eye-veins fire-engine
red. *"Chlorine for the germs. Fluoride for the teeth."* Belted in, they must have

followed instructions though the experts admit precautions don't matter.
*Aneurysm embolism-*stroke-stroke-stroke. *"Lay off the scotch and red meat."*

On Georgica Beach, blonde sisters dig down deep among the shattered
razor clams and hollow bits of broken moon-snails. Wood rot, hull and bone,

rigor mortis horseshoe crabs, buoys, one tennis shoe without a lace.
Whirly-gig flesh. Corpses—wind-blown across the mind. Divers dressed

like water rats forage long hours in the deep, as the search continues for
twenty cadavers and a voice contained in metal. Whatever it has to say,

no one ventures to predict, though the bloated toe revolving in a tidal pool
looked just like a hitchhiker's thumb desperate for the rest of its body.

ALONG THE CHARLES

Curves a path of shattered glass. Swans groom for the coming dark.
      Swans dreaming, swans asleep, a practicing
mystic fixed in a lotus, serpentine arms in a slow Tai Chi.

Cormorants perched on pilings dry their cruciform wings, though
      I measure time by blond, chestnut, ash,
the ponytails' swing of sweat glazed joggers wrapped in skintight lycra.

No thought, no mind, no need of hope. A swan's talc heart carried
      off by the blue crystals of the Charles. I find
a solitary bench and sit to jot some notes, to hold while letting go

of all the graceful strides of the lean athletic women I'm not meant
      to follow, the mind's arcane debris.
Rows of Harvard windows reveal students in their rooms

as they study theology and modern art, nestled in the halogen glow,
      heedless of the river's nearby doom. A sudden
chill where I stand between the pillared shadows. Everyone has

vanished and left me an echo of myself, below the frozen towers
      that rise into the light of deChirico. A coxswain's
rhythmic voice through a megaphone breaks in as I cross from

shoreline path to leaf blown street. Sailboats and gazebos
      penciled in a marble book. A hollow
boil-reddened, claw, hard torch in the pocket of my coat.

MARATHON

"And then you had the incident of this Swedish cartoons, which depicted Muhammad in the worst form, which is one of the worst forms of cursing Muhammad we have ever heard of. And then you now have the abuse of the book of Allah in ways that we have never heard of using it, as toilet paper and shooting at the book of Allah for target practice. So what is happening now and the enormous extent of it, even though it angers every Muslim, it is also a sign that the end of these kuffar [unbelievers] is near.'"
—Anwar al-Awlaki, from 2008 audio lecture from Yemen

In one region of Hell there are runners without legs.
Place your hand on your sweetheart's knee
and risk amputation by hacksaw or cleaver. Play
soccer and jeopardize losing a foot. Hum
in public and watch your tongue sliced from
your own throat. What can one do for the villagers
who will sway from the trees if caught dancing?

The immolated witches are remembered
at Olde Burying Point and judge Corwin's
wooden house, though the earth remains
fundamentally stone, especially for those left
bleeding, buried below a mound of rocks
and cinderblocks to preserve
the honor of kinfolk and neighbors.

Perhaps the lone true liberty resides
in cyberspace, where one is free to rant
and fetishize and find instructions on how to
build explosives. The bomb contained nails
like those sold at Home Depot
for residential construction, nails equivalent
to those deployed in the last crucifixion.

Still, one may observe the goodness of strangers
with numbers taped to chests and backs,
who gathered up the sweating, detached limbs
and sprinted them towards emergency vehicles
with their shiny white-red doors pushed open;
allowing at least some noncombatants,
to hope for an alternative salvation.

WEATHERVANES, CAMBRIDGE

The summer lawns beside the Charles are occupied
by undergrads working on their suntans. Pedestrians

unhurried pause to daydream on a nearby bridge. Some
carry wildflower bouquets, others clutch baguettes.

Kayaks cruise the billowed surface to practice linearity.
They're wise if they've discerned a route though none

have left a mortal trace. A russet glow begins to seep into
courtyard brick. Sunset on the riverbank glints on scattered

waste: bottle caps, plastic bags, flattened tin, cellophane
as Weld Boathouse windows are doused in garnet flames.

I see the dusk batik the irises of passersby and hear a broken
tuning fork turn beneath each sternum. *Rooster, eagle, iron gull,*

*puffed-cheeked god of the winds, Where to go with nightfall
pulling down the sails and calling all the runners home?*

The picnickers are folding-up their blankets and departing.
On horseback two officers trot below the small-skulled moon.

The last of Sunday daylight streams beneath the arches.
The concrete span cools and dims forsaken as a bone.

AS THE RIVER GOES NOWHERE
"I the apparition, I the spectre." —Walt Whitman

I've come to catch my breath to learn to breathe again.
My ploy of choice the Hudson wind
where pylons stand erect like pegboard pegs except
they're rotten. Beyond the barges Jersey City rises up like Oz
aestheticized in frosted glass. Joggers pant like Pavlov's dogs
amidst the Caribbean nannies preoccupied
with cell phone texts and steroid queers who pose
like muscled gods along the jetty. The sun
will croak within the hour beyond the grim refineries
and unprotected wetland grasses. Only toddlers'
glassy-eyed and belted-in to costly strollers are mesmerized
by the scuttling Chihuahuas. What exactly
is the message? Will I see it in the signage for *Premium Veal*?
On a billboard for a vampire film or a tumbler
of *Hennessey* offered as ambrosia? Patrons wait
impatiently to board a twilight booze cruise.
Barefoot martial artists turn their arms liquescent in octopi gyrations.
A row of stoic readers occupies the waterfront benches
cradling the covers of sun-warmed texts.
Everywhere I look another fine Samaritan with inverted
plastic bag is picking up a canine turd. I pause
to watch the romping dogs inside their chain-linked zone
with more time to cavort than gifted children.
Buoys strewn along the docks squat like bloated eyeballs.
I wonder, is this what our dead gods have become?
I gawk at passing pairs of spandex shorts stretched over peach-
shaped co-ed bums. The runners' strides quickening
to fend off death and look stunning in the clubs. *I turn
but do not extricate myself* as the final reader starts to shiver.
Like heroes from forgotten worlds, I'd rather perish
from within the greed for worldly love.
My shadow fallen on the river.
My shadow seeped into the tender grass.
The *whoosh* of passing roller blades all that's left of Hermes.

II

TRAVELING TOWARDS DAYLIGHT

The distance that separate us from the foreigner is the very same
that separates us from ourselves. Our responsibility toward
him is therefore but one we have to ourselves.

What is a foreigner?
A man who makes you think you are at home.
—Edmond Jabes

ABOVE THE CIRCUMFERENCE

Dreaming of the blue within. Sealed cup
of water placed beside me while I sleep.
After Vancouver the white hem of the Arctic,
angling south, skirting Pyongyang, passing
far above Pusan and Sapporo. The mind
bolted to a prior time zone, craving nightfall,
Valium, Melatonin while the nameless
continents rotate across my dozing eyelids.
Western Europe fully electrified, though hardly
an earthly star igniting the girth of Africa.
From Cairo to Johannesburg mostly undiminished
darkness, cluster of sparkly pinpoints
above Lagos, specks of paltry voltage
at Accra and Dakar. Inside my shirt pocket,
an embedded light rising from the flying eagle
emblazoned on the cover of my passport.

SINTRA SUNDAY

All the parking spots are taken near the market. Still
many have hobbled here with canes and metal walkers.

Strawberries piled high in boxes and garlic bulbs strung
into chains of hanging fat white jewels. Fruition here

even in winter. Lemons fallen in the plaza tossed about
by schoolboys. And whenever the wind gusts, hams

heavy as anvils sway with a solemn cadence above
the butcher's head. I notice a crowd has gathered around

a single cage. It's reason enough to have come,
though few of us can afford the price for such a songbird.

LISBON IN WINTER
after Pessoa

An old aproned woman with the stench of sardines.
The callused fingertips of men stained with years of smoke.
Vasco da Gama anchored in between the flaming tapers

in the hollow chill of See Cathedral. Two matrons shout
back and forth from half open windows, leaning out
above pots of withered geraniums. Below them,

a dapper man with sunglasses perched atop his head,
turns away to face a windless corner, to discuss local politics
on his stylish cell phone. Laundry has been hanging out

to dry for centuries. Maps of the sated left behind
on bed sheets, rinsed and billowing like glorious shrouds
above the cobblestones. Huddled over countertops groups

of jobless men sip espresso, da Gama not among them
to describe the unseen continents of heaven. A few bed sheets
always visible somewhere above. *Little dreamsails,*

towards which harbor, which world will you travel?
The answer etched in tidal stench: *Here, but not anywhere,*
tossing eternally trying to wake, groping for her absent

body, drifting scent of coffee, unread morning paper
folded on the sun struck table, bottles of port laid to rest
in a wooden crate, one atop the other like the dead.

Jesus, it is said, is never far. Jesus of the old felled olive-
wood, sanded and polished, then gashed and
gashed again, in the palms and in the feet by his creator.

FROM EVERYTHING A LITTLE REMAINS
after Carlos Drummond de Andrade

Bodies in the rain: riding trolleys, on the steps of banks and churches.
People running, covering their heads with newsprint, plastic,
packages and folding chairs, maps and sheet music
and cases holding tarnished instruments.
Nevertheless, *I walk towards death*
amidst the tangled flesh in the shattering rain.
On the wrong continent in the wrong language
I heard incessant weeping.
Emaciated Rastafarians with their Bonfim ribbons
waited beneath the dripping eaves. Mold,
sand, tobacco ash—damp and fetid. Myopia, fevers,
the blackness of visible nipples. Sweat, saliva, spittle,
ejaculate, drool—secretions all and holy.
In the middle of the road there was a stone.
Dead raindrops pelted the starless twilight.
The distant yelps of vicious dogs training for the underworld.
On abandoned street corners, women sold their bodies and offered cures.
Purity and charity buried in the volume of the rain.
I tasted the burnt yellow custard.
I listened to one guitar's transparent strings.
I stumbled upon the angel of memory at the bottom
of a derelict staircase while the night-clerk slept
with his forehead on the wooden desk
beneath rows of tiny cubbyholes each with its own silent key.
White legs black legs yellow legs.
Song-less rain. Droning rain. Rain—
the last translucent species hunting itself.
That implacable weeping followed me
as I walked beyond the afternoon, with fogged spectacles
in a sodden button-down, my canvas shoes
flooded like twin rowboats.
I wandered on through the stinging rain as if seeking
an otherworldly silence.
The crucifix by the ocean I mistook for an anchor.
This crystal watch broken into a thousand wishes.
Slouched and blurry I continued on through the tedious downpour.
A wooden birdcage for sale at the waterside market,
I mistook for the heart's indispensable prison.

POSTCARD TO PESSOA

Alfama hasn't changed much since your death.
The listlessness of aging whores languishing

below the crumbled archways. Each hat, each
pair of shoes, every hanging necktie mute

in each shop window, the paintings in the churches—
all too somber: the colors of smeared feces.

At five o'clock the downtown streets swarmed
by the rush and flow of trench coat shadows.

While outside the commuter's harbor another
lonely line of humanity waits to be ferried across

the river. For an hour I sat in your favorite café,
staring past your handsome statue. The site

of your immortal brain a resting place for pigeons.
I have one day remaining in Lisbon, time enough

to visit the carriage museum and another gaudy palace.
I can't speak a word of Portuguese. I have not

said a word to anyone today, and no one yet
has spoken to me. I lack fluency, though

at moments, hoped a beautiful downtrodden
stranger might approach and notice my head

buried in your selected verse. But no, the only
hands that touched my hands, wanted money.

LEAVING DRUMCLIFF

A long green tuft of moss divided the lone road. I chose one lane and went
away. Raindrops turned the hours into sound, tapping on my back and on
my shoulders while splattering the foliage. I almost offered praise before
a hawthorn tree, although I'd chewed gum nonchalant at Yeats' grave and left
with one good selfie: cold-eyed and thumbs-up. Waxen sheen of verdant
leaves pre-set to pierce all tenderness, reminding that each given crown
demands its share of blood. I nearly swooned beside the reedy shore.
Swans white as choir-robes, in love. I watched the duo sail away like words
That aim to range beyond but fail, the botched attempts at song. And yet
amidst adjacent clouds one seam opened briefly into sudden blue, sending
down a sunlit ladder to one small square of earth where I once stood.

THE INNARDS

The Troubles continue even if one excludes the inner life:
EU austerity and home foreclosures washed down

with the cheap milk of the dairy crises. Tractors plow
the agri-business fields west of Wicklow, north of Boston.

You'll have been amongst the last hands to scratch a bitter-
sweet dictation from capacious lands. Thank you for the tar-

black head of the mummified adulteress
who became my ersatz muse. Her voice that preserves

in me a bleaker hunger. I know of no one who considers it
auspicious to perish in their seventies,

though I hope the solace found in poems will continually
fill the chalices of untold moments. Potatoes are

a simulacrum, tokens from the innards. A wonder
given their multitudinous eyes and all of them, blind.

WAKING IN THE FOREST

In the dream I cradled the stone head of a horse.
I carried an injured swan.

I stepped inside the thatch-roofed cottage
where the blind harpist was born

and listened as he played
the words of Yeats and I turned weightless

as the feather of a wren, a grass blade,
a mica flake,

His harp: a simple wooden wing. I looked out
from his window as the meadows burned

kaleidoscopic green, then woke
dappled, alone in sunlight. *How our living bones*

attempt to mimic lucent strings.
The creaking towers of the pines swayed

like drunken gods above. I sat up where I'd lain
wanting to transcribe the vibrations

of the bees gorging on the loosestrife—burrowed
deep, and those firstborn songs of bards

and troubadours who held the dripping combs
that salve the heart.

SONG FOR OLD ROADS HOME

We took the lane beneath the archway in the rain. The path
ending abruptly as we paused to swill the dampened air.
Others far braver would scale wind-blown Crough Patrick
on their knees, for one must bleed untended to follow divine
will. The grassland hills densely packed with grazing sheep.
We kept a lookout for the fox who never came. Fences,
electrified and barbed were adequate, along with three yowling
dogs that nipped our ankles and leapt to set their forepaws
on our chests. Hunters too untamed to guide us while they chased
fleeter rabbits through the brush. What was it we were after there?
Memories of younger men who needed to believe that either art
or love might save them. Neither did in the end, but you had Christ
and a forty-year wife, who every now and then lay breathlessly
like the Pieta across your lap. I ludicrously strained with ever younger
love while burying a mother and several manuscripts unpublished.
The pubs we haunted in the '80s and tapped our feet iambic
through many night-long sessions have all been refurbished
for the rugby fan and those who rather fancy to sing-a-long with
Mumford or Adele. Guinness now poured polar-cold as Coors
and Bud, and Corona widely advertised with posters of Cabo
and Cancun. We parted outside Boyle. You had a nursing home
appointment. I bought a discount ticket to the abbey ruins where
plastic falcons placed on sills dissuaded local birds from crashing
into glass at break-neck speeds. I never did write to you about
what I'd discovered there: a disembodied shepherd preserved
in bas-relief on one squared Cistercian stone. One jutted forearm
flowing into fingers that enclosed an upright crook that rose
straight until it curved and spiraled inwards at the top like scrolls
of fiddles rarely heard these days in country inns. Fist and crook
restored for touristic scrutiny, for those who've stopped to break
the flatland journey between Dublin and Yeats' grave. I stared
wistfully at this one collection highlight: a calm hand bordered
on all sides by nothingness, as it held on for dear life.

LAST CALL

I lost my way on the road to Coolmine—after The Palace, The Long Hall,
after The Bleeding Horse, somewhere between the Blanchstown Mall
and the Castleknock Dog Pound. I glimpsed inside Bacon's studio
at scattered imagery and piled texts: *The Book of Monkeys* and *Diseases
of the Human Mouth*, Velasquez popes and Van Gogh sowers,
iridescent carcasses and the unsheathed histories of decomposed lovers.
Afterwards, I met Pat for a couple of pints. He expounded on reverence
and the ephemeral. I discoursed on the grim chasms in time. Our glasses
raised and lowered like the sea tides, lowered and raised like our aging
bodies humbled before the Communion. We toasted to our cross-pond
journeys, the pulchritude of muses, the pennywhistle's tiny grief's
and the bodhran's ardent certainties. The session music playing unabated,
made even more resplendent by the *ping* of one string, breaking.

AT SANTA MARIA TRASTEVERE

Gypsies circumambulate the fountains,
selling fresh-cut long-stemmed roses.

Industrious vendors seeking those
effortless to spot: the gloss that ripples

from the forms of newfound lovers.
St. Francis too embraced the thorns,

every agony that burrows—each green
nail that stabs then sprouts the humane

in the heart. *The Ecstasy of Saint Theresa*
required no explaining. I stopped

for Corvo Rosso in a dream. The carafe
refused to empty even as I poured.

A flower-seller ambles over
to where I dine alone, al fresco.

Let me place
one petal

on each
eyelid

then teach you
how to mourn.

WATER IS ONLY ANOTHER NAME FOR TIME

He napped beneath the oxidized sundial, its porpoise fin
risen to the surface. Bees rummaged in the nearby clover
filling his jet-lagged mind with the hewn gold of honey.
While overhead, the passing Redwing blackbirds draped him
in diaphanous shadows.
                        Crossing Italy by train, he watched
the glistening olive groves while she slept, or read Montale
aloud in a whisper even though she would not hear him.
However far we've stumbled from the source a trace
of the sea's voice will lodge in us.
                              They adored the languor of ancient
fountains, the moonlight spotlighting the narrow brick streets,
the lone bronze girl in their hotel courtyard, diligently filling
her pitcher as a mob of gleeful cherubim shot streams
of water from their mouths and urethras.
                              There were dawns
he'd been wakened by their splashing, dawns when their cadences
would lull him back to sleep. Night will fall within
the hour. The timekeeping porpoise already plummeted
down into the lower ocean.
                              Before sleep, they'd look down
at the goddess below their window. And without saying,
understood: water is only another name for time. How her flagon
continually filled to the brim then spilled over, as if insistent
the emptiness, which mortals so revere is impossible.

BELONGING

On Main Street America each block is its own principality
for those over twelve and under twenty-one. Skateboard slackers

rule one storefront stoop. Another nearby corner is governed by
metal-stud punk rockers with hair dyed lilac, verdigris, fuchsia.

Even the melancholic gothic-pale in flaccid clothes that drape
their waif-like frames, guard a portion of concrete, fingertips

rolling cigarettes with an apprehensive calm. Though in Narni,
it's the aged not the young who come to the piazza

in the sultry twilight to sip *Campari,* puff cigars and banter
about the latest Bertlusconi antics, rolled copies of *La Repubblica*

discreetly tucked beneath their arms. Nobles of the Duomo stairs,
their gazes fixed on hilly distances, on meadows of poppies

along the old road to Spoleto where each wound-shaped blossom
recalls an ally's valor. Those who've outlived Mussolini gather here,

wheeled in aluminum chairs by wives or nurses. Men, who like
myself, tilt their heads slightly back to watch the pigeons trace

circles on the sky, and listen to the feral ones mating hungrily
above the heads of gargoyles whose eyelids have begun to crumble.

BLINDNESS AT MADANEK

I arrived mistakenly, one hour before the official opening,
though the main gate was already unlocked and swung wide.
Employees in pairs tooled around in golf carts. A security guard
lingered beside his mountain bike, smoking a Viceroy.
On a pathway separating meadows, an old woman hobbled by
with a bucket of yellow flowers. A fancy green tractor turned
back and forth, cutting hay in a nearby field. The prisoners
made art from dirt: a giant tortoise—its neck elongated from yearning
and a castle with moat and towering walls forming a world
that was impenetrable. I walked amidst the shimmering maples
toward the lone brick cylindrical chimney, but found myself
looking beyond the barrier at the smokestacks on the far horizon
employed for mundane industry.
                                                    Returning to the entrance
I noticed a pair of wire-rim glasses dangling from a wooden railing.
Not the sort of eyeglasses one would use temporarily for reading
or distance vision, but lenses one must wear to see at all.
How might a man misplace a pair of spectacles, which rests
upon his wakeful face? I wondered if he'd left them intentionally,
not wanting to gaze outwards any longer or as a caution
to other visitors who would follow. Crows, white butterflies,
ragged shoes and ashes. Soon the youth would arrive by the busload.
Israeli flags rippling amidst the barbwire. A few dogs
growled at who-knows-what from apartments on the peripheries.

AFTER TENEBRAE

"O one, o none, o no one, o you" —Paul Celan

I read your poems on half-empty buses from Brasov to the Polish border.
Slept in the district where Elie Wiesel lived as a child and toured
his modest house with its sky blue walls as if our first dreams might persist
or be revived amidst a gentler humankind. In Paris you wrote
"God pray to us." But to whom, to what, in that netherworld should've
I addressed? The Jewish graveyard had no other visitors that morning.
No uniformed guards were in sight. Nothing but a fenced-in square
of damaged headstones submerged in muddled undergrowth.

Your voice rose through me on de-feathered wings with guidelines
on how to touch the eyelid that occludes the sun, a method to interpret
those lost voices cowering among veils of falling snow. What was
there to reclaim as I walked the length of another pogrom town?
I watched a gaunt shepherd drive his flock through an unlatched
metal gate as the lone word *herded* tore off inside me like wool-wisps
on barbed wire. *Herded,* herded how quickly they were *herded.*
Once terrified then horrified then shattered in the learning to obey.

FURNISHED ROOM
after Herbert

In this room are two suitcases
a bed not mine
a scarred wooden dresser the odor of torn off evergreen bark

A mottled brass doorknob and damaged lock
the desk's varnish stripped by scissors and penknives

Corner chair heaped with woolen blankets
one lace doily decomposing as if woven by drowsy spiders

Only the far wall
an outdated map of the world
the Arctic like a skullcap worn by a pious Muslim world

continents oddly formed into fake shields of Achilles
nations with outlines like Ajax jigsaw puzzles
whose borders are rarely faultless

no plate on which to serve my darlings
no glass vessel or ceramic jug for water

There's a small library on the bottom floor
where others have vanished inside some other's words

At the end of the fetid hallway
a bathtub with the feet of the Sphinx

A ship's porthole that is a mirror
in which the sea sees itself,
one wave lit shrilly by one naked bulb
summoning each guest to an endless horizon

THE VILNIUS CHRIST

The cathedral square is treeless,
blanched cement baking in August weather.

Nearby, a shady park with benches,
a Via Dolorosa lined with alpine trees.

A weary half-pious tourist,
yielding to the wretched heat,

I almost turned away. Though
once inside the bone-white cathedral,

I was met with gusts of air-
conditioned air. And there

above, spiked to shins
and palms, his kindled wings afire.

NOTE TO RITSOS

When I was last here, you were alive and time was standardized
as BC and AD. Soon that might change and we'll demarcate Greek
life as BE and AE: *before and after the Euro.* I hope

Greece will be dirt cheap and cheerful again; back on the drachma
the waitresses flirtatious, the ouzo flowing, the cod laid out
like horizontal trophies glinting on the Mykonos docks. Your islands

awash with Kiwis, Swiss, and young Israelis needing to stay high,
shattered from their duties on the Hezbollah border. Years ago
stoned hippies more audacious than me, colonized the seaside caves

draping their corrugated floors with handmade Turkish rugs. Although
I suspect it's the jobless locals who can't afford the German rents
who lodge there now. Daily rioting below the Acropolis, youth refusing

to imbibe the hemlock of austerity. How it would pain you to see
these corporate cannibals with their hunger for hard currency—
easier to digest than the tendons of the lamb. Years ago on Syros

I savored the salty winds, the shadows of wisteria etched along
the white-washed walls as the old widows passed head-to-toe
in black. How they seemed beyond mourning.

SCALES

On sidewalks bordering flea markets and bus depots, pensioners and widowers
sit the whole day, before their antiquated scales, waiting for some passersby

to weigh themselves for little more than a penny. An adult human brain weighs
thirteen hundred grams, the average heart-weight a mere ten ounces. Still

most of us will fail to admit the heft of life is incalculable. One only need observe
the sun's buoyancy in the moments before nightfall, balancing on the ocean's

long horizon, to stand and brush the sand off, then turn away from the dimming
waves, to hear, faint and weightless, the breeze of one's own passing.

WHEN THE LIGHT IN DREAMS IS IDENTICAL
TO THE LIGHT IN DEATH

I'd just returned from a bus tour of the mass graves at Baba Yur
with an hour stop at the Chernobyl Museum with its photographs
of a radiated humanity. Thyroid cancers, gross deformities, rashes,
workers in protective suits raking, shoveling and tossing out debris
as if performing mundane yard work. On the road to Pripyat, we
passed deserted farms and in town center amidst derelict apartments,
the driver spotted a wild boar foraging beneath a rusted Ferris wheel.
Neither images of genocide nor toxic-leakage disquieted me more
than Tommy's disembodied voice. His body shelved in a Bangkok
morgue, kept cold for an upcoming autopsy to rule out overdose
and foul play, while I lounged in a three star hotel in Kiev with beets,
blinis, herring and crème fresh on the breakfast buffet. That night
I slept with the Archangel Gabriel hovering above the rows of empty
contamination suits till wakened by an almost inaudible voice, saying
I'm alone now. Outside my hotel window I count seven construction
cranes and the golden domes of two Orthodox churches. Tom never
said goodbye and neither did I. Poor connection? Lost signal? Does it
always end like this? Or had Tom, by sleight of language, reversed the
pronouns to make certain that I knew, I didn't want to be alone either,
which is precisely what I was: a tourist within easy reach of lingering
radiation and anonymous piles of Jewish bones, following the hush
of his words. Watching the summer dawn through a fifth floor picture
window, scanning the hilly, tiered horizon. All these unfinished
buildings pocked and skeletal like honeycombs abandoned long ago.

POSTCARD FROM ODESSA

The widow selling sunflowers at the bus depot has quietly departed
while the man with the sad accordion played to the coming darkness.
A gruff drunkard demanded I hand him Euros and a shapely coquette
offered to entomb me in her ravishing body. Though mostly I walked alone
unnoticed along the promenade, heeding the guttural whispers of need
and desire. A veneer of moonlight tinted the Opera House wall near
the circular fountain that shimmered obsidian. I'd watched sunlit children
there that afternoon, wade-in and splash with an unselfconscious joy.
Gogol wintered here near a statue of the hoisted earth stippled with stars.
I'll be leaving by mini-van tomorrow. *Time just drives the horses on...*

SABBATH OF THE SUICIDES

I've seen them rinse their feet beneath cold faucets at dawn. A crucifix
tethered to a pilgrim's wrists and those who followed, singing. Tourists
at the Wailing Wall appear well fed, wear fine linen. Designer labels

our latest gods—no wish for redemption. A voice blares above the old city.
Bow, stoop, drop to your knees. I don't know the word in Arabic for *sin,*
but the tone admonishes. You must cover your hair, your breasts, your lips.

To pray you must open your pocketbook, let the soldiers search for bombs.
Stoning's and protests, immolations and laments. Rosemary redolent in blossom
among the tombs. A chalice sealed in museum glass never to be sipped from.

THE SAME DUST

The Israeli Air Force sky-dropping leaflets:
Evacuate now with your donkeys and your goats.

Vacate with your tattered Korans and rusting teapots,
your satchels of unripe figs and torn posters

of Mecca. Another chilling night, watching
CNN as rocket fire blisters Palestinian skies,

as bombs strafe Gaza and smaller mortars hail down
on Sderot, where underground, concrete "shelters"

are re-named "home." Who can know for certain
whom the righteous are: the rock throwers

or the builders of bulwarks? I want to speak
with those children kneeling in the street,

but they're mostly quiet, mesmerized by
the puddles of blood that decant so smoothly

from the human skull. The night sky from afar
might appear to hold an unspeakable beauty.

Munitions arc overhead like comets and shooting
stars or other supposed celestial truths.

But haven't we seen the truth remains elsewhere,
always with the earth or buried in the tombs

of saints and martyrs that no one hears clearly.
One might sense this when crossing the border:

how the dust that powders the tops of our shoe
is the same on each road, dust without

an anthem or a flag, dust beside the nameless
groves abounding in oranges and olives.

And how at their separate weddings, they dance
the same way: with arms raised to the heavens.

OSTROVSKY SQUARE

He sits amongst contented strangers, outsider in a foreign park.
Old wood benches enclose dense beds of red and white petunias.
A bronze hero on horseback trots triumphantly ahead. He will
never recall his name. Tajik, Uzbek, Kyrgyz, Chechen—amalgam
of bitter dialects with occasional, pitiless laughter—all a babel
to his ears. He watches others pass beyond his makeshift day,
their gestures yielding to less ambiguous translation: children
gripping ice-cream sticks as they prance across the gravel, hands
waving at video cameras, the quick two-checked kisses of greeting
and departure. He pretends to read his *Lonely Planet*. An alien
to those who've gathered here, if not for the solace offered by
pigeons. The *snap* of wings in ascension everywhere the same.

-Saint Petersburg, Russia

IN THE CITY OF RIVERS AND ANGELS

Most of the bridges were small and he would cross them
in ten steps or less: towards the light or away from light.

Mokya   green waters.   Gibrodayev   braided river grass.

He was gazing at the angels poised along The Hermitage roof
when schoolchildren released myriad balloons like punctuation

deserting the sturdiness of sentences. A broken clock above
Nevsky Prospekt. Lovers outstretched on the lawns

of the Summer Gardens. He stood indecisively, an overused
map half-torn in his hands, while burly laborers hurried past

with their fresh-cut flowers: white-and-yellow lily bouquets
carried upside-down like torches pilfered from the underworld.

Guided only a portion of the way, no one offered to instruct him
how to offer a bouquet so it led to a lover's bed. Though the hotel

desk-clerk cautioned him, "the mosquito coil fuming all night
in your room might induce perplexing dreams." At dusk,

he lurked amidst the crowd gathered beside the *Fontaka,*
watching as an oxidized stallion netted in a mesh of blonde

human hair was hauled like a shipwreck from the bottom.
Later, in an unnamed square, transfixed by the unremitting sky,

he noticed other angels tremble on their ledges. Stone bodies
that fell in slow-motion, tumbling end-over-end till they flew.

ON THE FIELD OF MARS, AFTER NAPPING

He wakens on an empty lawn
to the bells of St. Isaac's.

The park lamps in daylight
glowing faintly amber.

Above the treetops, Chagall
bouquets drift by

in the outstretched arms
of angels. On earth,

rose petals dapple a pathway
with little blood-footprints

and pressed into soft dirt
the shoe prints of unseen gardeners.

On the far side of the park
a bridal-train ignites—

careening like a dragon's tail.
He walks peaceably

through the slowness of twilight
towards the intricate canals

where the lilting waters purify
the long bones of the moon.

-Saint Petersburg, Russia

DOGS IN ORBIT, 1957

Laika launched from a Soviet boondock
when Mother was one month pregnant with me.

Genius bitch that perished hours after lift-off
from over-heating, stress and barking at the cosmos.

The lonely orbit that childhood was.
I've never really grasped where I am headed either.

"Behave like a person" Mother often chided
for I'd howl, bark and whimper whenever she left

me behind. Only the serenest females who needn't
lift a leg to piss, reached the rank of cosmonaut.

A SHORT HISTORY OF FLIGHT

Tracking small birds through the wind-swayed catkins:
wren, swallow, sparrow.
I drew their feathers thickly with crayons and built small fires.
I searched for nests. I named myself *Hawk.*
I carried a dead crow home through the charred gates of childhood.

The difficulties, which obstruct the pathway to success
in flying-machine construction
relate to the construction of the sustaining wings;
to the power required to drive the machine through the air;
to steering of the machine after it is actually in flight…

The young Amelia Earhart climbed trees and hunted rats with a .22 rifle.
On December 28, 1920, pilot Frank Hawks gave her a ride
that would ultimately transform her life.
"By the time I had got two or three hundred feet off the ground," she said,
"I knew I had to fly."

Mother never said a word when she caught me touching myself.
Father was mute about desire.
At age twelve. on a summer tour boat of Alcatraz Island
around the time of my first wet dream, the guide
speaking though a megaphone expounded on the birdman's history.

Mother pulled white tissues from her handbag
and wiped my fingers clean of melting Ghirardelli chocolate.

                               Though Issa understood:

Children imitating cormorants
are even more wonderful
than cormorants

In his efforts to pare down the plane's weight, Lindbergh left behind any item
he considered too heavy. These included radio, parachute, gas gauges, navigation lights.
He designed winged boots. Instead of a heavy leather pilot's seat,
Lindbergh perched in a wicker chair.

Describing his descent into Paris
I saw there was a danger of killing people with my propeller and I quickly
came to a stop...I was astonished,
it was like a match lighting a bonfire
To sidestep other "issues" I'd begin a psychotherapy session
with some ludicrous question.
What is your opinion of Matisse's cutouts, especially
"The Fall of Icarus," (1943).

More than once during the prison cruise, mother reminded me,
this is where the naughty boys go.

Charles Augustus Lindbergh, Jr., twenty-month-old son was kidnapped
about 9:00 P.M. on March 1, 1932, from the nursery
on the second floor of the Lindbergh home near Hopewell, New Jersey.

In the two-and-half-years before his Atlantic crossing, Lindberg Sr.
parachuted four times to safety in harrowing emergency situations,
earning him the nickname, "Lucky Lindy."

I'd often speak to my shrink about art because I was certain
she was as bored with me as I was with myself.
You must be familiar with Hopper's Mobil Oil Pegasus in "Gas," (1940)?
Like Hopper, I deemed motion as antidote.
"Maybe I am not very human," he once remarked.
"What I wanted to do was to paint sunlight on the side of a house. "

In 1966, after three identical ranch houses were erected on former swampland
at the end of Fairfield Road, I had no asylum left in landscape
and needed to figure out how to vanish within.

Bury yourself
in a book, mother would badger.

Some afternoons I played astronaut,
covering my skull in Reynolds Aluminum
                    then blasting off for Venus.
                    Or try to walk weightless as Christ across Saturn's rings.
During some of the long wordless psychotherapeutic pauses,

I'd attempt to guess what my analyst was thinking:
how my dreams of flight were nothing more than a disguised wish
to fornicate. I was gladdened when she concurred
with my free association—
the waste of post-masturbation semen
like Icarus wing-wax melted near the sun.

There is another way of flying which requires no artificial motor.
I refer to the soaring flight, by which the machine is permanently sustaining in
the air by the same means that are employed by soaring birds.
They spread their wings to the wind, and sail by the hour.

Hendrix and Joplin shared a fondness for feathered boas,
in that they closely resemble wings.
To dissolve the self by placing a tiny wing upon the tongue: *blotter*
Mr. Natural, Purple Haze, microdot.

"I don't know whether I believe in God or not..." wrote
Matisse. *But the essential thing is to put oneself in a frame of mind*
which is close to that of prayer."

Known simply as Bear,
the grandson of Kentucky Governor, Augustus Stanley Owsley
served eighteen months in the U.S. Air Force during the 1950s.
In 1967 police raided his lab
and impounded several hundred thousand doses of LSD.
Despite this incriminating evidence, Owsley claimed it was for personal use.

A white streak behind him flowered out into the delicate
wavering muslin of a parachute—a few gossamer yards
grasping onto air and suspending below them, with invisible
threads, a human life, and man who by stitches, cloth,
and cord, had made himself a god of the sky.

In 1909 Stroud was pimping his girlfriend in Alaska and gruesomely
bludgeoned her john who refused to pay. Locked up at McNeil Island
penitentiary, he assaulted an orderly who reported him
for trying to obtain morphine.

At Leavenworth, he stabbed a guard to death in the Mess Hall
in front of eleven hundred inmates.
It was there Stroud developed his interest in birds,
after finding three injured sparrows in the prison recreation yard.

For hours I'd play Vietnam airlift by myself,
levitating the exhausted, inch-sized action-figures above the plastic palm trees
as my giant, gym-ripped G.I. Joe stomped across the ravaged landscape.

My therapist inquired on more than one occasion as to why I
persisted in talking about my favorite TV shows from childhood
rather than my mother's terror or my father's taciturn hostility.

In springtime I sat with Ian in the basement of Guggenheim through
six straight hours of the *Cremaster Cycle*. Leaving the theater, dazed at twilight,
I was only able to recall those scenes involving flight:
the two blimps carrying their cargo of grapes,
the naked male body covered in scurrying bees,
Jacobin pigeons in the Budapest Opera House trailing satin ribbons,
the Chrysler Building soaring on its pinnacle at midnight.

After combing 250,000 square miles of ocean,
the government called the search off.
                         In 1938 on Howland Island
                         a lighthouse was erected in Earhart's name.

A flash of lightning:
Into the gloom
Goes the heron's cry.

I'm inside the spiral of the Guggenheim Museum.
I'm waiting on the runway, my skull framed by a small cold window.
All the runways remain frozen from Nashville to Dulles.

During the assessment of the kidnapping scene, the police found traces of mud
left on the nursery floor. The body of the kidnapped baby was found partly
buried and badly decomposed, four-and-a-half-miles from the Lindbergh
home, forty-five feet from the highway, near Mount Rose, New Jersey.

I exchanged talk therapy for pills when the therapeutic couch began to feel
like quicksand. I have a tall orange vial of Prozac.
I'm happier, fatter and a bit impotent.
I keep a black and white postcard of Matisse in his wheelchair thumbtacked
into cork above my desk and quotes from one of the Apollo crew:

> *It suddenly struck me that that tiny pea,*
> *pretty and blue, was the Earth.*
> *I put up my thumb and shut one eye,*
> *and my thumb blotted out the planet…*

Beautiful, beautiful. Magnificent desolation.

I saw *Wings of Desire* for a second time at the beginning of the 21st century,
at the Film Forum on the last Tuesday in December.
Heather and I walked out from beneath the dark marquee,
slack-jawed, nearly breathless.
It was ponderously snowing as the city re-emerged
in black-and-white.
Each one of our steps left a fresh boot print in the middle of West Houston.
Parked cars entombed beneath fresh snowfall.
Yellow taxis skidding south on 7th Avenue towards the tunnel.

We both admitted how during those last two hundred minutes
we'd taken turns falling asleep.
I scraped a handful of snow from one windshield and tossed it in the air. You seemed so
joyful in your silly pom-pom hat, putting on your rainbow mittens.

Stroud was allowed to breed nearly three hundred canaries and sparrows
in two adjoining cells, conducting research that became: *Diseases of Canaries*
and *Stroud's Digest on the Diseases of Birds*. While he wrote on Death Row
his mother repeatedly pleaded for his life and Woodrow
Wilson pardoned him.

I kept one wing positioned over my eyes and spent my adolescence stoned.
My understanding of cosmology based on re-runs of *Lost in Space*.
The teen years a misty blur: *nitrous, hash oil, 'shrooms and Thai Sticks*.
My bong longer the length of telescope allowing me to peer at other spheres.

I'd obsessively watch re-runs of *The Munsters, The Jetsons* and *The Flintstones*
and discerned there the truth of family life.
I embraced the compassionate machismo of *Johnny Quest*
and *Speed Racer's* homoerotic languor.

We haven't yet departed.
The glum pilot informs us "there are still ten planes ahead of us."
I want to ask for a cup of water but feared the flight staff's scorn.

I pass the time imagining a beautiful arrival: the last scene
in the history of one flight.
That sense of hovering just above the earth three minutes before landing
when I'll behold the whole of Manhattan as a vast electrocution in gold.

In 7th grade algebra class I was awestruck:
how every girl was simultaneously developing breasts.
It was around the time of the first lunar landing,
I began to touch myself in earnest and lost interest in everything else.

SAND THEN GLASS THEN MIRROR AND THE GIVEN LIGHT

I'd walked half the length of Nevsky Prospekt when I glimpsed
my jet-lagged face staring back at me from a taxidermist's window.

Miniature fox, flying squirrel, lynx, badger and within the glass
between us, my perplexed countenance, as if I'd become a minor

character in a Turgenev story. A hunter in the nightfall forest,
suddenly lost. In Ostrovsky Park, I watched a drunkard sitting

on a nearby bench, attentively pour sand from each of his shoes.
First one shoe then the other shoe. His gaze fixed on the taupe

granules suffused with sunlight, suspended momentarily in the air
before him. I passed the taxidermist's shop later that week

and once inside, inquired about a creature with tiny skull
and elegant antlers that spiraled like antique sconces. But how

would I explain to U.S. Customs my peculiar fetish for the head
of a rare Russian rodent? I stood with two elderly women

waiting at a bus kiosk, muttering to themselves. One wore a red
vinyl raincoat to rebuff the solstice sun. The other stood poised—

a regal matron with an admiral's cap. I began to notice others
out for a leisurely morning stroll, wearing identical white naval

hats rimmed with black and gold. And wondered whether
this haggard fellow emptying his shoes, had only just returned

from a windswept beach, and if others here were equally
possessed by the longings of northern sailors: for sand to break

free of its hourglass, to burn in the constant fire of summer,
becoming glass, then mirror, then a place of self-shimmering.

PAGAN AT GARNI

The plaque beside the temple explained the pagan worship
of dragons, later effaced with intricate crosses, then obscured

by Arabic script proclaiming this edifice officially a mosque,
then re-conquered and re-christened as a church for the next

one thousand years. The statues of the goddess were prostrate,
shattered. I looked on dismayed by the diktats of justice,

of faith vanquishing faith. On the road after Garni,
a young woman beckoned me to taste the ripened cherries

from her orchard. Her hands bulging as she reached across
the wooden fence to pour the copious orbs into my cupped palms.

The sleekness of her calves, pale lattices of her ankles, her
firm figure stretching upwards from atop a wooden step ladder

like a goddess upon a tall pedestal. The lovely cadences
of her slender arms as they swayed among the plentiful limbs.

SUMMER ABOVE DEBED CANYON

Armenian cheeses, plain yogurt, straw-colored honey in a small
ceramic pot. Combs like porous bricks set dripping on a plate.
Bread, eggs, butter, roasted pears, noodles. Everything locally
grown and homemade. Blackberries, raspberries, peaches, apricots
stewed in their own viscous syrups. Peach preserves yellow-gold,

apricot jam burnt-orange. Boysenberries bobbing lusciously whole
in tall glass jars. The owner of the home proudly watched me
devour breakfast, then disappeared inside the house, quickly
returning with his Russian-English dictionary, two shot glasses
and a liter of vodka. Though nature soon required less of language

as we stood after one-too-many-*nostrovias,* on the balcony over-
looking his garden. He pointed at each bush, shrub and crop row
crammed into his modest yard and proceeded to label each life
like the first man given God's instructions. Peach, plum, apple, pear,
gesturing to various trees in succession. Thyme, dill, chamomile,

lilies. The strawberry patch, plots of cucumber and haricot verts,
the underworlds of potato and red onion. About the mushrooms
and berries, he turned away from his yard and swept his arm far
and wide, covering the forested hillsides behind his village—
Odzun, to be sure I understood the garden beyond the garden.

TWO MARKETS: UZBEKISTAN

I. Samarkand

An Uzbek crone pursues me through the Siyob Bazaar.
Her headscarf designed with birds of prey alighting
with gnarly outstretched talons, her gold teeth flashing
crookedly demonic. She cradles an infant underneath
one arm and carries a satchel of freshly cut dill. *Why
is she trailing me between the stalls of butchered mutton,
into the section of candy vendors selling brown-sugar confections
in chunks the size of geodes?*
                              Instead of music, women
grating beets and carrots for fresh fermented salads
sound a vigorous strumming. Before I know it, I'm face-
to-face with this gurgling, blue-eyed baby raised to
the level of my eyes. The crone speaking rapidly
in Tajik. Her chaffed pink, open palm extended. I point
to the dill, buy two bunches then briskly shake
the fragrant bundles at the level of her infant's curiously
widened eyes, whinnying like a gelding as I walk away.

II. Tashkent

In the spice pavilion in Chorsu Bazaar, my brain begins
to shiver with pleasure. Fifty-kilo sacks of turmeric,
cumin and coriander, the pale green sails of bay leaf,
the crinkled, night-dark pods of tamarind. Spice dealers
frantically waving their arms, calling unabashedly, *Hello!
Sir! Mister! Boss! Hello! Hello!* One or two men whistle
shrilly, compelling me to turn my head as if something
colossal was at stake, more than the ordinary seasoning
of lamb, beef or poultry, or garnering a few extra *som*
from overcharging a naïve tourist. Their insistence
implying that merely by carrying these regional roots
and leaves, dried and pulverized through U.S. Customs,
I could waken an entire nation to elemental desire.

RUMI RETURNS TO MAZAR-I-SHARIF

It is also Afghanistan's unofficial capital of prostitution— so much so that "going to Mazar" has become a byword for Afghan men looking to pay for sex.
—The New York Times

        to consider writing love poems for the 21st century,
to whirl in the streets—a lone dervish preaching the bliss of dust,
to search for scarlet lips blousy as opium poppies in springtime.

Is it possible to recognize innocent singing after a massacre and reprisals?
Muffled radios in clandestine rooms to occlude the virile groans
of pleasure. The youngest of the divorced and the widowed

on their backs, their gazes fastened to ceilings or posed
on knees and hands to keep their coffers filled with Afghanis.
What would Rumi intone now? Eight centuries ago he noted,

the soul sometimes leaves the body then returns, though this
is also relevant in coital trauma. While other of his lines reside nearer
to a psychiatric truth: *our nakedness together changes me completely.*

Is it two conquering forces: the Taliban and U.S. military, or four
powers, if one includes divine and mortal love? Rumi fled the onslaught
of Genghis Khan in this same city, then grieved in exile mutely

for decades over his murdered teacher. Loss shadows us through
the world then leads us away from the corporeal. The ruins of the old
khanaqa still standing where his father taught and he studied as a boy.

The BBC reports: if you visit Mazar-I-Shair today, you still might
meet a few local men who ecstatically chant his verses, if they haven't
yet been slain for recitation of profanities. Rumi praised sweet wine

and the grapes from which they came, the gardens and the roses
that compose them, but that was in his other life in Turkey.
I wish I knew to whom and about what he was speaking, when he said:
     There's nothing worse than to walk
     out along the street without you.
     I don't know where I'm going.
     You're the road, and the knower of roads.

DRONE LAMENTATION

US reconnaissance missions crisscross
the furnace of Saharan air.

But do these mechanized eyes rightly differentiate
nomadic caravans hauling salt
from squadrons of radicalized Mujao?

And why are drones baptized *Reapers*
when fright is what they sow?

A Western headline reads "Reapers in Niger"
like a horror film title that sends an ample scare.

At a press conference, African and French ministers
of defense express appreciation for these 56.5 million dollar
terror-seeking-&-repellent eyes

while village elders dig graves for their daughters
and their sons whose heads will face towards Mecca.

TERCETS FOR TERRIFIED LOVERS

The chocolatiers are shuttered. The florists
instructed to slit their long-stemmed roses at the throat.
Toy shopkeepers must eviscerate each huggable bear.

Clerics declare:
remove *all heart-shaped cards from your shelves, all balloons,*
all sweet-filled boxes. Craven are the images of mortal love.

Valentine the martyr was not a Mohammedan martyr.
He healed the blind, kept epileptics from seizing, spared
beekeepers from stings as they harvested their hives.

Indignant men swarm the Kohat streets. Fists clenched
raised up against Western lusts. I pray no one
will see you kiss or hear you whisper in Pashtun

Darling
Sweetheart
Honey.

Valentine's Day 2016, Kohat, Pakistan

GRAVEL CHILDREN'S SONG

All our roads are falling down,
falling down, falling down.

Rubble, mud, roots and rocks,
no way to ride from town to town.

We live in makeshift shacks and huts
or crawl beneath blue tarpaulin.

Too many nights completely dark,
no candle flames or kerosene.

From morning birds till rising stars
we break the stones, break the stones.

A child's game we make it fun
and don't complain or whine or moan.

We know our chisels aren't nice
from Home Depot or Fisher-Price.

All our roads are falling down,
falling down, falling down,

strewn with mud, twigs, rocks and roots,
no way to ride from town to town.

Once a year a monk stops here.
There is no real virtue in pity.

We do our puja. He imparts:
a mind serene as stone is free.

ONE DAY, MAHABALIPURAM

I. Dawn

On palm-lined residential streets, mothers and daughters kneel
outside their homes in the concord of early morning.

I listen to the tinkling bells encircling their ankles
as they trace the vivid symmetries of fish, birds and blossoms.

*Chalk drawings arranged for the gods who adore
the colored dust and whatever will become of us.*

II. Noon

Sand in woven baskets across their arms, sand in metal buckets
steadied upon their heads. Gaunt women in saris work construction,
back and forth and back through the midday swelter.
I wobble along dust-roiled streets in a heat-induced daze,
wishing only to enter the vellum leaves of an illuminated book,
where hallowed lovers loll within their hedgerow garden,
inhaling jasmine, feeding each other apricots from silken fingers.

III. Dusk

The chink of chisels from roadside shops:
metal on granite, the chipping of flint.

A massive Shiva sanded by eight simultaneous hands,
clothed in a placenta of its own dust.

The spirit guardians who defend the Shore Temple
have been effaced by briny winds. Thus

the task of mortal work: re-reveal the almond
of each eye, the spiral of each ear, carve free the Nandi

bulls from their granite thrones, that they may fly
off—away on the chariots of sunset.

THE RIVER AND THE WHEEL

A Hindu priest explains the blessing of the earthly flame
and the inauspicious karma of those the government must cremate.

"The corpse is laid on huge electric coils. It's quick and economic
especially in this holy city with its scarcity of proper trees."

Above the cremation ghat at <u>The Home for Women Aged and Poor</u>,
crones not yet arthritic, darn throughout the day to save sufficient rupees

for their wooden pyres. While other widows ravaged by TB,
merely lift a palm and plea, longing for a body burning down.

*

Along the Ganges, shoreline launderers lounge and doze
while festive gold and purple silks that swathe
the richest of the dead, peel back, then off like ornate snakeskin.

The soul released as dripping fat. Jasmine,
saffron, sandalwood—its sweet and final condiments.

Not a single mourner hides their gaze
or weeps even as the inner fluids boil loudly over
and the epidermis sputters till it *pops*.

*

Men urinate wherever they want—
any wall or scrawny shrub will do.

The body incarnate doesn't matter, while the *true*
self-perceptible within the inner mirror

is revealed as an incessant beggar.
I notice fellow foreigners

donning orange robes, eating only
rice and dal, then assuming transcendental poses.
Behind me on the mendicant line

a voice gently urges:
This alabaster elephant is a sign
of lasting happiness.

You must smear some yellow
tikka on its head.

Go to him. Go
with paste and petals then bless yourself.

*

Touring the ancient crematoriums I'd worked up quite
an appetite but after three days running of tomato-onion
curry, all I could negotiate for lunch was a glass of warm chai
and a moon-sized antacid. I meandered in among the post-
card stalls, dodging mounds of cow-shit and prostrate,
gray-bearded sadhus with open palms awaiting Euros.
The mood in the market was upbeat. The Indian army had
recently defeated Pakistani rebels in the Kashmir snow.

In a trash-strewn lane, a lanky teen accosted me
to explicate *The Indian Way* - "not only giving to charity
but shopping for rugs and silks will bring you excellent karma"
—insistent as he coaxed me towards his uncle's shop.
On our way we paused before a devotee of Vishnu
who stood sublimely with his trident, demanding fifty rupees
per snapshot from a portly group of tourists, each seriously
posed for their Hindu versions of "American Gothic."

After being led on shopping sprees and erroneously
into shady rooms for the purchase of contraband antiques,
virgins and hashish, I decided the finest karma I could hope
for was not to die in Varanasi, let alone, alone in the *Hotel Ganges*—
a one star guesthouse with fearlessly inert cockroaches.

AMONG THE HOLY

The memory of bone-smoke that flagged Gandhi's pyre
more than forty years ago is a slight, eternal flame.

Nearby, in another time, lean and lanky men engulfed
in greasy fumes are grilling goat and mutton.

A black marble slab inscribed in Sanskrit exclaims
the human right to hustle, honk, and tailgate, lie down

on any street and perish, seek alms outside the air-
conditioned mall and beside the ruins. I arrived in Delhi

with a wad of rupees in my money-belt for hailing cabs
from holy place to holy place: the Lotus Temple

to the Lakshmi Narayan where a goddess drifts forever
in a sea of blood-red petals and comforts those who've lost

their wages at cards or dice. I walked among the vendors
below Jama Masjid: cheap shoes, mangoes, dried fish, steaming

chai and plastic toys, Peddlers with potions, gelatins and
powders, the unemployed whom the snake-charmer blessed.

Pearl and ivory inlay, fine Islamic tile, humbled human forms
on their own straw mats, writhing supine, waiting. Clubfoot,

leprosy, an array of amputations amidst the pandemonium
of businessmen with spells and secret remedies. The resonant

voices of the pious rising through the traffic din. Their righteous
cries to Allah, frightened pleas for rice and bread.

THE COCHIN DAWN

As the dawn arrives on the narrow shore, he walks to the harbor
to watch the boats unmoor and the dexterous fingers of young men
unknot nets, and the low clouds—peach, pink, orange and gold

no longer ethereal, but hulking across the sky as if strung along
an abacus upon which he counts his loses and counts again,
the days that still remain for him. Crows tyrannize the seaside,

perched by the hundreds like miniature vultures on stone walls
and electrical wires. He wanders several yards then stops among
the watchful eyes of rickshaw drivers, dock workers, touts and

would-be tour guides sipping chai at two-rupees-a-cup and joins them
with his own tiny beveled glass, unconcerned with water-borne
illnesses, savoring the traces of cardamom and heavy sugar.

The sound of the street-sweeper's stiff straw brooms in unison—
labor given only to untouchables. What about his vision of untangling
this life—freeing the self, foregoing the body for a consciousness

loftier than a Bangalore high-rise? Cheap rooms, cheap cuisine,
an affordable enlightenment. He envies the beaded foreigners
adorned organically from head-to-sandal in white or orange muslin

and those who breathe effortlessly with an ankle twisted behind
their necks. Some of us are not that flexible and love complaining
in French, German or Hebrew accented-English about the service or

the fees. But who is here to serve whom? Too many deities with various
answers. Too many stone bodies inside the temples on which to drip
ghee and daub *tikka*. He watches intently as the chai-maker pours

each cup in an arc across the air. The speed of liquid retaining its flawless
curve. A little magic as brief as the eyes opening each morning.
Ceiling fan whirring like helicopter blades, the heart nearly taking off.

COLLECTED WORKS

The world scoured
by mop, broom and rain.

Landscapes fallow
as the moon, as my mother

fretful without her wig
between the chemotherapies.

As I traveled north
from Leh towards Srinagar,

the women gradually
hid themselves. First hair,

then lips, then the eyes
dimmed like two winter suns

beyond shapeless clouds.
My mother's collected works:

keep the house spotless,
play competent bridge.

And recently added to her list:
staying alive for my father.

What is this veil
between you and me? Where

is the bridge on which
one might cross back?

A first edition hardcover,
glacial and untainted

in the middle of a crowded shelf,
pressed on both sides

into obscurity.
While within the poems,

nothing hidden
but the end,

which in itself
is an endlessness.

-In memory of Agha Shahid Ali

OOLONG

Morning fog lingers until
it burns off.

The arrival of clarity
entailing substantial time.

He enters a labyrinth
of tea plants. Nothing here

is linear: neither roots
nor paths, nor the murals

within the temple
of coiled serpents

or the elephant tusks
ornately carved

like the instruments
of gods. He knows

that he is nowhere
to be found, but doesn't

mind. The air is
fulsome with dew.

He pauses before
a path-side shrine

where ghee, freshly
dripped upon

a faceless stone
divinity gleams

with the sunrise,
as he often

wishes to, and
sometimes, does.

CLOUDS AND THE WHITE ARMS OF COMPASSION

Wind-shredded prayer flags flutter above the Ura Valley.
Whatever we proffer is never quite ample:

bruised yellow apples,
yak butter for the altar lamps,

a few lesser banknotes
with the serious face of the king.

*

The cliff-side
pines concealed

by fog, nearly
vanished.

*

Void outside, void
within. East of Trongsa,

reclining Buddha
in gold leaf

dreaming of a time
outside time

when another human life
might waken.

THE MINGUN BELL

The second largest iron bell on earth is spattered with graffiti,
which did not prevent me from having to pay the three dollar
"Archeological Zone Fee" for the privilege of beholding another

defiled artifact. This bell no longer rung with purpose, struck only
by foreign tourists willing to pay the requisite one *kyat* to take
the wooden mallet from a schoolboy's hand, who's turned his day-

long truancy into an occupation. The robes of child novices flapped
like wings in the riverside breezes: nuns in bright pink, monks in dark
cranberry. They accosted me with their wooden alms bowls

and basic English, asking "where are you from?" Had I'd been
a wise ass, I might've answered, *which incarnation are you referring to?*
Instead, I gave them most of what I carried in my daypack: two pears,

one samosa, some small denomination notes. I gazed into their sinless
faces: expressions neither disheartened nor elated, while ruby-dappled
generals oversaw the trafficking of laboratory heroin and old-growth teak.

A sudden monsoon downpour! Soldiers and villagers all scurrying
for shelter. Only the robustly plump stone Buddha sat unmoving
in a rain-soaked lotus, chortling as the law required, without a sound.

THE COMFORTS OF AMBER

Smoked fish hang from wooden racks along the shoreline road
to Lake Issy-Kul.

Bodies split. Gills partly open. Trout,
perch and pike oily to the touch.

For sale at the higher elevations
glass jars of apricot jam and wild honey in golden variations.

Women wrapped in floral headscarves,
wave their fleshy hands
beseeching passing cars to pull over.

What was and what will be, matters less.

Three months from now our bodies heavier, encumbered.
Skin turned the color of jarred paste

as we drive through mountain snow
past frozen lakes, wind gusting its Soviet-era radiation.

August: sunlight ladling the day.

Melon rinds and tiny, intact skeletons nonchalantly tossed
from rolled-down windows
on the summer road to Bishkek.

Only fish-smoke lingering pungent on fingertips
as if in advance we had touched our own pyres.

THE ONLY FIRES

Each night in Lhasa, Dave and I took our supper
on the rooftop of an Indo-Tibetan restaurant close
to Jokhang Square. A knowledgeable Buddhist,
he tried to keep me straight on its lists of saints
and deities. We assumed, our waitress who told us
she'd migrated from the countryside, subsisted
in the capital, meagerly on tips although it was her
gentleness, not the quality of the mock Tandoori
that brought us back each night for Kingfisher's
and earnest chat. She gave us her email address
to keep in touch and before leaving for Pokhara
we stopped at an ESL school to enroll her for she
wanted to learn more in a tongue she equated
with freedom. Years later, when the first riots flared
we wondered how she was but Google, Yahoo
and Hotmail were shut down and all we knew
of Lhasa was what we'd read from half a world
away: of curfews and travel bans, of farmers,
monks and nuns dousing themselves in diesel
and setting themselves aflame. Whatever Dave
had once explained about each monastic lineage
I've long forgotten—gone-up with the flesh-
smoke of activists and dissidents, their holy-
orange robes roiled, wind-blown, blazing.

MY SHANGHAI DICTIONARY

It's safe to say I would have been completely lost without it.
I noticed the locals glancing at me—suspect in this Caucasian
epidermis, as I pulled a thick bi-lingual dictionary from the pocket
of my daypack to plot my next move along the Bund.
There was demolition everywhere. Wrecking balls pounded
like temple gongs. Towering construction cranes—rose up
like metallic flowers—the latest symbols of resurrection.
Paralyzed, without a word of functional Mandarin, I could hail
a taxi but where would I end up? I couldn't shape my mouth
to form a plausible sound. The unused muscles straining
and quivering around my jaw and throat. Pound kept several
Chinese dictionaries in his cell at St. Elizabeth's. I carried
his Confucian volume, <u>The Great Digest & Unwobbling Pivot</u>
(1951), in my suitcase to present myself to myself as *literate,*
though I barely read more than a few pages the entire journey.
This dictionary, a now frayed paperback enabled me to find
the railway station then board the right train for the Suzhou
Gardens. A handy lexicon also after nightfall, for ordering
crab sautéed in ginger, minced pork and jalapenos and asking
a college student majoring in English to step with me onto
the dance floor then perch at the edge of my hotel bed and
open her mouth slightly and press her lips to my lips till our
dialects dissolved in muffled vowels, and assist the uniformed
guard who led me through the cavernous museum to the suits
of Tang Dynasty armor layered densely as the scales of giant
reptiles and into the room of Ming Dynasty vases with their blue
and yellow variations that the emperors equated with heaven
and I equated with the taste inside her small pink mouth.
Nonetheless I often lost my way, entering a transsexual massage
parlor, served a bowl of cold, translucent jellyfish. How does
the saying go, *make no mistake—make no mistake about it.*
I smiled and I paid or I smiled and ran for my life.
Next time in Shanghai, I will carry a dictionary powered by
double-A batteries that speaks correctly but robotic. Paper
usurped by electric current or as Pound translated the link
between obsolescence and beauty. *Oh fan of white silk/clear
as frost on the grass-blade,/You also are laid aside.*

60

THE FIRST MAN FALLEN IS THE LAST MAN STANDING
Study of Perspective- Tiananmen, 1995–2003 —Ai Wei Wei

It wasn't art or magic:
the lone civilian in Tiananmen Square

who immobilized
an oncoming tank

by lifting
a single hand.

Imprisonment then banishment
by virtue of having

raised four fingers and a thumb
in calm defiance.

*

The middle digit slightly curled
poses

questions concerning free
speech and justice

while summoning forth
those

who once believed
they lacked courage.

*

The clout
of one finger. Stout

symbolic warrior
held upright

in a defiant *fuck you*.

Fuck you to tyrants
and oppressors.
Fuck you, even

during torture,
even after

breaking.

BASHO AND TOGOE AFTER THE LITTLE BOY

Flocks of white geese, flocks of white cranes—
…before…after…One lurid cloud
roiling aflame. Not a moment to surrender.

On a distant mountain, in his humble cabin
a nameless monk sweeps
cold cinders from the furnace of history,

sweeps from his mind's-eye
the countless eyes aghast,
blinded by an unfathomable light.

For those whose flesh did not peel instantaneously
away, *Togoe wrote "Give Back
the Human."* But how to give to those

whose skin was smelted,
enduring thermal burns, leukemia,
melanomas, ulcerations, convulsions.

The world remains explosive:
Kalashnikovs, grenades, car bombs, landmines, drones,
flung rocks, hurled stones.

Few rowboats anchored among the moonlit lotus blossoms.
Few friends still adrift, sharing wine and verse.
No black-crowned heron's love song for the dark.

In a world of one color the sound of wind.

62

S-21

Inside every renovated cell: shackles, rusted bedsprings,
one automotive battery to administer shock. I follow

a tour group of hip Scandinavians through the rooms
of the former elementary school. Each teen adorned

with at least one piercing: eyebrow, chin or tongue. A dragon
breathing fire from a bicep, a python encircling a wrist.

Needles enjoyed by choice but who can blame anyone
for wanting to serve as a billboard for transformation and rebirth.

Prisoners were often burnt with a lit tip of a *Marlboro*
or drown in a soup pot used to cook Khoy Teil. The horror felt

by others isn't easy to assess when staring at the snapshots
on the walls of those who perished. The Khmer Rouge kept

excellent records. The street outside Tuol Sleng unpaved,
sun struck, roiling in dust. A vendor stands beneath

his colorful umbrella with soft drinks, juice and bottled water.
I watch a Frenchmen heatedly haggle to save himself

eleven cents. History written in transparent ink: tears
attached faces, tears attached to names, though the market

stalls not far from here are lush with life: spring onions,
bean sprouts, leeks, chilies, cilantro, bok choy, lettuce.

BENEATH THE DISCO BALL, PHNOM PENH

A midget sits beside the neon gates, eyes me through
    a cheap tobacco haze. Behind him cans of beer stacked up
        to the ceiling, each with its own snarling tiger. *Don't worry*

friend, he says, *I'll tell your cab to park and wait between*
    the kiosks where pork and dog are charred on skewers
        and flames are madly leaping. He propels himself forward

on a rickety toboggan. I follow him through webs of red
    and purple strobe to a darker realm where rows of girls in
        taut pink miniskirts and numbered badges wait, and skulls line

the shelves in rows above their heads, each one tagged and
    numbered with month and year HIV was contracted. *Have*
        no fear, insists the dwarf, his lips pressed to my ear. *They were*

merely children—too young to consciously suffer . You know
    now why I've brought you here: immortalize this fusion
        of sex with death. Scribble in your little notebook. Hold a Tiger

by the can. This realm must be a paradise for poets. There's
    always several girls and skulls unlabeled, whom the bard at
        his leisure may inscribe later. One girl moans, another pants

with her thighs apart, while the bored dwarf chain-smokes,
    picks his nails and sniggers. The pus-bright sun rises up
        on shot-glass, flesh and bone. Out, out, out, we flicker.

OUTSIDE MY WINDOW ON A TRAIN TOWARDS DANANG

All the scarecrows in the rice paddies
are faceless and diaphanously white.

Four decades after an unconscionable war
and still slowly following behind water buffalo plows.

Old farmers and their old seed-sowing wives
who'd watched the rainy season skies

for bombings, and not
forgotten.

THE PORNOGRAPHY OF NAPALM

The child running naked never stops running, never breaks
her stride running towards us. Crying *nóng quá, nóng quá*—
too hot, too hot. Remember she was naked not because she was
impoverished or bathing in the waters near Trang Bang.
Her blouse consumed by flames as she ran from the bombed
pagoda with other village children howling. She is moving as fast
as she can along the dirt-rut path away from her home, away
from the scorched rattan huts, the burning trees, from the burials
to follow, US troop withdrawals, treaties, ideologies—away.
Her skin flayed and oozing as she runs from the woe her body
has become. Seventeen operations later, scarified yet still alive.
Migration, marriage, motherhood—a lifetime lengthy enough
to somehow forgive. Her Facebook page without one selfie showing-
off a haircut or designer shoes while counting each thumbs-up.
Fifty-three years in terrified flight, certain she is dying as she runs
unstoppably towards us, shrieking at the top of her lungs: *too hot.*

for Phan Thi Kim Phuc

WORLD MUSIC

Saigon after midnight: inside *Apocalypse Now.*
A bar-girl wearing cheap spandex brandishes a pool-stick,
flirting with her newfound mates from Melbourne.
                                        The barstools

are all occupied by lithe, talc-faced girls
decked-out in flaming hot-pants or old-world Chinese silks.
They glance from time-to-time at their imitation Swatches
as if waiting for an airlift to a milk-and-honey nation.
                                        Over rounds

of ice-cold Heineken, a clan of shit-faced travelers discuss
their recent visit to the *War Remnants Museum,* though no one
cares to mention shell casements in the countryside
converted into planters for eggplants, scallions and tomatoes.
                                        My friend,

it's a brand new century. Whichever way you wander
you'll meet a limbless beggar while the music of Madonna,
Dire Straits and Sting pours onto the nighttime streets.
                                        Beat your swords

into ploughshares, slip your condoms on. It's closing time.
Last dance. Last call.
The DJ spins. The patrons sing, *"WE-ARE-FAMILY! WE!"*

LUOI

In the Mekong rain, longan and mangosteen
dripping in the orchards: sweet on the tongue, sweet on the tongue.
South of Cantho on my Honda Dream

past rows of karaoke clubs. "Mista, what you want? Mista, what
you look for?" Bored young girls perch on plastic chairs
below auras of pink neon. But I only want to rest with you

in the unknown touch of sleep,
on a cloudy morning, in the Mekong rain,
longan and mangosteen sweet, so sweet, on the tongue.

TRAVELERS OF THE DREAMLESS HOURS

A crone standing inside a bamboo kiosk, stirs *arroz caldo*.
Only faint electric light on the back roads in the Palawan
pre-dawn from the few garages vulcanizing rubber
lit by dim fluorescent tubes. A florid scent unfurls
across the valley and I know myself as fortunate
being even half-awake among the lolas totting baskets
of taro root to a distant market and young men in blue-jeans
and fake Ray-Bans, dozing in weary reverie of beauty queens
and cock-fight bets that win ten thousand pesos. Even
on this rickety, hard-bench bus, sitting in between
a puking toddler and a voluble veteran unhinged from years
of Ginebra, who reminds you every twenty minutes
of "the greatness of America." With the dawn is a luminous
hue of papaya, we travelers of the dreamless hours
are as far as they will ever be from home. *Child, little one,*
sway back to sleep. Soon the sky will reveal its torches
and the coconut palms will suddenly appear on the long
horizon, majestic as the columns of the Parthenon

MANHATTAN/BALI: A JET LAG IN FRAGMENTS

"Under jet lag…something deeper is dissolved… you lose all sense of who
and where you are…You feel like an exile, a fugitive of sorts…" —Pico Iyer

Dawn light on my eyelids
The *clop* of law enforcement horses
Smooth motion of a trolley suitcase rolling through a terminal under renovation
Menorah of smokestacks
Vibrato of hummingbird wings
The canceled and delayed arrivals of sleep
A Boeing 767 floating towards the borough of Queens
On a white ceramic plate a brown pool of peanut sauce and six sticks of chicken satay
An immense square hole—just dirt in between two buildings
Where the bombs exploded
Nusa Dua Nusa Dua
Fire hydrants like midget amputees
Goldfish visible then disappearing swiftly in echoes of concentric circles
Rain in the waking
Rain before sleep
A taco truck parked on West 14th
Mannequins dressed in *kamben* in every storefront window
One small banana leaf-box filled with rice grated coconut and one red
Bougainvillea blossom
The detonation here
The attack there
Sound of a pizza being sliced into eight isosceles slices
Women adorned in yellow-gold walking in a long straight line
Trays balanced on their heads with piled symmetries of mango and apple
"Are you carrying anything fresh, live or lethal?"
Velvet ropes and beyond them only a single rose for sale
Cantankerous monkeys guarding the shoreline temple
Tentacles of sautéed octopus like the infinite arms of Shiva
A Customs form with rows of empty boxes to X or check
"Honey, please rub some sunscreen on my back"
Kuta Kuta Kuta Ubud
Fire escapes lined with potted geraniums with petals the size of Christ's stigmata
Gods with expunged faces
Waves churning and frothing beneath the Whitestone Bridge
Oysters inside their marble tombs on crushed ice at the raw bar

Green shadows of feeding cranes in the fields of *Peliatan*
Bouncers with guest lists where men with bloodstained aprons once stood
Dismantling lambs with chainsaws
The aircraft rising slightly during its descent
Canines in rabid packs patrolling unpaved roads
Tinkling bracelets encircling the ankles of dancers where I also heard the sea
A pair of winter boots unoccupied outside each apartment door
One brown leather mangled glove palm-up on the sidewalk
Wet footprints impressed in beach sand vanishing upwards from below.

WEATHER & TRAFFIC
after Szymborska

By mid-afternoon it will be a real scorcher.
Humidity will climb to 99%
inducing sopping armpits.

The sky from Wall Street
to Ellis Island
will loom partly cloudy

composed mostly of cumulus ships
that will explode
without a sound.

Haze galore
and as usual, poor
visibility.

Take some time
to catch your breath
for the air-quality is suspect

and of no concern to Exxon/Mobile.
Pressure, whether low
or high will emanate

from within. The breakdown
lane on the LIE
is already overcrowded.

Expect a rage-inducing wait
at tollbooths. All city bridges remain
indeterminately under repair.

Thankfully the setting sun will dispense
gilt rays that will reel and jig
on the dance floors of both rivers.
Low tide will carry a dreadful stench
and high tide, a hazard
to Baptists and surfers.
A late evening drizzle
sheer as Christ's shroud
will paint small rainbows

where motor oil dripped
on asphalt, so be sure while walking
to look down.

The sun like a punctual guest
is expected to rise
at 6:35.

Tomorrow should be noticeably
better for those who don't rely
on alarms for waking.

READING WALLACE STEVENS ON THE METRO NORTH

At least a few commuters must have lingered longer at the office,
met a friend for cocktails, walked away early from a bad blind date,
endured a muted therapy hour, took an evening class at NYU
or Pace. Copies of the *Times* cradled under arms unread
though it's practically tomorrow.
The 9:52 to Brewster North. *He rode over Connecticut*
                              In a glass coach
                    The hour neither: late nor early.
The riders facing backwards gazing stupefied, straight
into the space from which they started.
Faces hollow-hardened by what they face.
A slice of pizza on a lap,
a wrap in whole wheat pita with alfalfa sprouting out one end
like some unruly garden. *And there I found myself more truly*
                              *and more strang*e.
                    Framed by one dark window
a woman skimming *Vogue.*
High priestesses with airbrushed noses
while Harlem from this height appears poorly lit and broken.

Bodies now diminishing toward the dissipation of the day.
Each one of us mutually alone, watching hairlines
vanish or scalps turn mausoleum-white and pigeon-gray.

Make partner, make a mint, make a splash that lands you on page 6.
Men with loosened neckties seem more at ease than most,
having paid most of the mortgage off
as the brain slowly expunges sex with death. *Out of my mind*
                              the golden ointment rained.
                    The therapist laments
if only he could heal you with idioms of moonlit glass.

Why must one fight to keep awake? Katonah…Purdys…Goldens
Bridge…Unconsciousness is gift and test.
The feeble dreamer's mouth forms O.
The drool, the snore, the cough, the virus transmitted by touch and breath.
One must have

A mind of winter
Although I'd rather dwell within
the languor of his Key West visions. *The world is ugly*—no,
                                    I can't finish.

Sleep is fragile refuge, our waking and our wake.

SWEET EMPTINESS

              With the on-coming traffic halted by stoplights
          I paused mid-avenue to look up at the wide corridor of sky.

Cloudlessness, the absences of seagulls
and pigeons, no Homeland
                                        Security drones to blemish
                                    the vastness of azure.

              It was the quality of daylight
          that roused such sweet emptiness

like that summer twilight
in Yangon
                                        as I watched other tourists
                                    practicing compassion.

              Others like me, who'd purchased
          one caged sparrow

                        then
                        released it

while agile teenage boys with nets
clambered out along the branches
                                        to re-capture the same birds
                                        to sell again tomorrow.

IN HUMAN RIVERS

I. LEGS

AND THEY'RE RUNNING

running in their Reebok's their Asics their Saucony's running
    with their I-Pod's MP3's and Blackberries their cell phone plan
    with unlimited minutes and playlists longer than the 10,000 things
    inscribed in the Tao Te Ching
they're running in spandex breathable cotton tank tops golf hats
    bare-backed bare-chested some with tattoos, murals
    some with dogs—dogs ahead behind beside the pure bred
    pedigreed Border Collie Bichon Frise Labradoddle Whippet
    Standard Poodle groomed like labyrinthine shrubbery
they're running for their lives to look better in the boardroom bedroom
    on the dance floor in the mirror gasping sweating grunting
    as if one could make exhausted love with oneself
they're running with their newborns their infants toddlers half-
    legal adoptees from China Ethiopia Belarus Honduras
    their in-vitro twins saddled in designer strollers
they're running one assumes away from death away along the river
    while others chose to march and pray to sit and sing refuse
    to move in Zuccotti Park in the freedom to be still and gather
they're running through daylight savings time time saving saving
    time a belief in amassing the disappearing hours
    collectible as postage stamps Nikes snow globes sea glass
    while others run towards God pedometers wrapping biceps like tefillin
No one seems to notice the anomalous walker immobile because
    he's exhausted afraid of failing falling out of breath breathless
    while the sun sprays shattered gold across the Hudson
For anyone bothering to look at all closely would've known
    he'd fallen that something fractured tore or broke within him
but they're running running running running and the only others pausing
    seek to lessen the lactic acid build-up to stretch and stretch out
    pressing palms against a wall or railing as if suddenly apprehended
    for a nameless crime patted down and frisked by un-seeable detectives.

EASTER 1997

By the steps of *Our Lady of Guadalupe* aroma of warm tortillas wafts
Holy trinkets for sale at the kiosk: plastic Virgins and pewter crosses

tying Christ to rearview mirrors. Little girls in strollers, dressed as snow
white princesses wheeled past mauve petunias in ground floor window boxes.

Outside Port Authority a teenage mother in skin-tight jeans and carmine
heels pauses as her daughter waves to drowsy upright rows of silhouettes

arriving here on Greyhound buses. Widening days, this lavish light. *First
Tupac, now Biggie—it makes no sense.* All the hopeful hymns have finished

while every prayer I never said, is the image of a fragrant lily my mind sought
to become. Chocolate rabbits wrapped in pretty tin, watches guaranteed for life

strapped to vendor's wrists from Abidjan and Port Au Prince. Sunlight wedged
in blockish shadows on worn facades on Washington Street where couples

stroll with shopping bags, the wistful sway of those in love. Although
it's Sunday and the meatpackers are shut, the mortal scent of butchering.

SUNDAY BRUNCH

Long sidewalk queues
of the annoyed, aggrieved, impatient.

If one didn't know better
one might think the masses

are tediously awaiting rations:
salt, bread, oil, milk, a butchered rasher.

ONE DAY IN THE LIFE OF A BENCH IN CENTRAL PARK

The uniformed schoolboy hastily stops (it's almost eight—
he'll soon be late) to assess the contents
of his *Batman* lunchbox—then runs off.

    *

A young mother happily bounces her cherubic daughter
on her lap, then nonchalantly undoes the topmost
buttons on her blouse.

She offers the soft volcano of her nipple
up to her gaping mouth. They *coo*
together like doves with the morning sun upon them.

    *

Skipping out of high school the teenage couple
sit rapturously close. They kiss
gently then fiercely then gently again.

Pausing, they watch a squirrel scamper up the trunk
of a thick-barked oak, then gaze
straight ahead at the yellow-white beds of jonquils blazing.

    *

Nearing the end of his eight-to-four shift
a park employee dressed in a pressed beige jump suit

leans his rake beside him like a friend
then proceeds to read and write text messages.

    *

Silver earrings twisted like Mobius Strips',
leather mini-skirt, high-rise-white high heels.
Friday after five implies it's *Happy Hour.*
A young woman pauses to evaluate her lips.
Pulls a bullet of lipstick from her purse
and a compact whose mirror shares its roundness with the earth.
She makes two swift claret swipes, brighter than a cardinal's wing.

*

In the outstretched shadows of sunset, a gentleman carrying a briefcase, a raincoat slung over the crook of his arm, stops to reflect (as if he might've left something important back at the office) then starts rummaging through folders and files, such that one consider even in this wireless era the significance of paper:

certificates of birth, passports, report cards, parking violations, antiquated
pay-checks, marriage licenses, leases, wills, divorce decrees, restraining
orders, proofs of purchase and vaccinations, visas, diplomas, graduation
speeches, homages, sermons, eulogies, homilies, wedding toasts, certificates
of death, moving violations, the faces on the 10-most wanted list.

The man abruptly turns and walks back in the direction from whence he came.

*

Near nightfall the park-lights go on automatically
and begin to glow.

Bronze halos
doting the mostly empty pathways.

An elderly couple takes refuge here.
They appear

unafraid
despite the parks status as "unsafe

after dark." They
hold hands
while neither speaks. Maybe
they're thinking *how*

one must die first.
Or maybe, they're waiting for the owls.

SUBWAY 7AM ABOVE THE EAST RIVER

The mornings commute without desire.
Bulky forms cocooned in winter coats.
No seats left west of Jackson Heights.

I'm forced to stand encircled beside the closing doors.
Odor of black coffee stale on someone's breath and the mustiness
of another's damp, shampooed hair.

From the bridge above the river a sapphire sky
arches overhead. Below, sparkling sunlight
bedazzles the flowing surface of the water.

Those absorbed by ear bud music or a glossy magazine
I suspect must be pretending. Wellness granted
mostly to those engrossed in small-print texts,

which insist *the toll for our iniquities is to fall,*
then live fallen. I watch an elderly woman zigzag one finger
down the pages of her bible, riding snug amidst

a babel of strangers with their downcast shifting eyes.
Eyes, darting here-there-here-there as if searching
for a mislaid talisman, an ingress to this fleeting light.

DOWNPOUR DIPTYCH

Puddle formed
on asphalt street.

To human legs—
a nuisance:

to cross,
traverse.

step around,
skip over.

In a quiet
later, devoid of

cars, delivery
trucks, pedestrian

cell phones,
emergency vehicles,

a pigeon comes
to rinse

his feet,
sip

fresh rain,
ponder

new-
found mirrors.

II. AMONG GOLDEN WINDOWS

THE PIG RIVER CARRIES WITH IT TWO LINES FROM DU FU

What's the honest difference between a nose
and a snout, between a *yum* and a *grunt*
or the pink of pig bristle and the flush of
human skin? Outside Shanghai, countless
bloated bodies float along the Huangpu,
the latest grim image of a world coming
to its finish. *The sorrow of riverside blossoms
inexplicable,* as Du Fu presciently noted
thirteen hundred years ago, while we're
being held in the long arms of our two
Manhattan rivers. We order-in moo shu
pork, shrimp lo mein. Eat from waxy paper
cartons, upright on the rumpled bed. Later,
I'll wear my hog mask before we make love.
It seems the hills and rivers have been waiting

CLOSING TIME, TORTILLA FLATS

Shot glasses in an orderly row like pawns on an invisible chessboard:
Patron, Herradura, Chanaco, Corazon. Sean and I too drunk to feign
connoisseurship, more concerned with the stunning blondes
in short black skirts, perched on barstools, crossing and un-crossing
their legs in a kind of soft-core genuflect. With *Love Shack* blasting
from the stereo and the Christmas lights blinking lustfully
in all the windows, Sean leans over and mumbles, "almost heaven"
and I don't disagree. The lubricated mind coasting across the clear
thin ice of *anejo.* Their legs, we've overheard, beach-tanned
in the Caribbean and slickly shaven, with the remaining few
extrusive hairs succumbed to hot wax. *Yep, just about perfect, except
for going home alone,* walking east on Bank Street, pausing at the corner
of Hudson and Bleecker, to inhale the night-chilled gentians.

THE DISTANCE OF UNKNOWING

I stand looking out from my bedroom window. Each
un-shaded window is a crate of light. A square set
on vertical boards for a game yet invented. Before bed
I watch others framed by their own windows, backlit
in the gilded distance; gazing out through the sooty glass
to forget what time held and disgorged, to fill the vapid
space with strangers in their own rooms, though I can't
discern if they're women, men or adolescents, if
someone is holding a kitten, a baby bottle, a cell phone,
a can of beer; if others are also looking at the moonlight
brushstroke the Hudson, the tugs of passing clouds,
the few seeable stars over Hoboken. I live at the distance
of unknowing, and will never know if anyone
has turned to look inwards at their own unchanging
walls as someone they'd still loved, walked away.

TWO MEN ALONE STANDING NAKED IN THEIR WINDOWS IN THE DARK
"I want people to be afraid of the women I dress." —Alexander McQueen

Coastal Maine with its vast mussel-shell beds:
crushed whirls of off-white and bleached indigo

returned him to Alexander McQueen and that dazzling
dress composed of cobalt-silver shells

fastidiously stitched together and spot-lit in the MET,
titivating the genderless model in the radiant.

*

Notable is the splendor of the uniformed warrior,
the glistening necessity of armor.

McQueen perceived beauty as a fallible buffer—
hanging himself six days after his mother's death.

*

The poet too falls inwards on the failures of song
to lessen distance. His mother

already dead now for seven years.
Still, he sings to her

and of her, so to live
without her.

Oh mother, mother of pearl,
clothe me in your moonlight again.

ODE TO THE PILLOW

No one knows who invented you. If your first earthly form was carved
wood or stone or if you were an avian gift arrived as a book of feathers.
Your shape stolen from the tablets carried down by Moses after heeding
the voice within the fire. Your body is sea foam, white as a rabbit's silence.
Two sugar cubes attached to each other's sweetness. Mother often said
sweet dreams, as I say to you love, for our pillows are snowbanks, clouds
freed from gravity, ghosts of taxidermy owls. Still one must live inside
your erratic nightmares: of doves that flew off in peace but didn't return
from the war zone. Fears of blackboard chalk that all truths are erasable.
You, who accompany the supine one-third of our earthly hours and
beds for our dogs that lead us home from exile, for the dog who rescued
the winged-boy who'd tried to reach the sun. Faceless are your clocks—
their numerals falling off one by one as one approaches eternity. You,
who are nearer our breathing than any clinging lover. You who retain
the terror of marble, which is soon to become the Pieta. There's no
resisting your lures, the glaciation of sleep. The only species to survive
in your landscape are the unicorns and lambs whom the gods continue
to watch over. Pillow hoisted horizontally—our first and final sail. Vessel
that is able to transport us daily into the center of the earth. Pillow
I purchased on the lunar surface where I paid with the light of my bones.

III. SONGS FROM A TIMELESS METROPOLIS

MY DIZZY GILLESPIE

I was never *hip*. Never
cat or *dude* or even *man,* prefixed with
Hey or suffixed with *What's up?*
I wore a generous beard years back
but looked more like a lumberjack than an upright bassist.
Not quite *hot*, not quite *cool*
but wanton for a impervious calm, a natural chill.
And I'm hardly *a brother* to anyone, even my flesh and blood.

Watching Dizzy at the Blue Note in the last years of his life,
I was seated at a table with Japanese tourists.
Chic felines in short black skirts, in black silk tights,
with satin-dark eyes and silk-stream hair, framing
their alluringly pale faces. And all of whom ignored me,
even as I leaned suavely back in my chair,
a plaid beret occluding my alabaster bald spot.
The music dazzling, a perfect
complement to a noxious mix of loneliness and lust.

How Dizzy drove his breath with the pleasure of a mouth
at the breast. Returning center stage
for solos, stepping out that night, as he does
at unexpected moments from his side of the grave
for an elegant rendition of *A Night
in Tunisia*. Though I still can't say
what music is missing in me.
What lost song.

APPEAL TO BLUE TRANE

Traveling steadily away from myself, wayfaring
steadily away. The rotund moon, blue

clouds, blue ice, blue frost, blue tower windows
where I remember being,

being beside you, beyond the blue of solitude
and the searchlight of memory.

I follow the moon, another wounded moon, blue
memory and the searchlight of solitude.

Blue vapors, indigo smoke, cobalt cries of the river-
birds flitting above the steel-blue waves.

Your horn is a lighthouse, its flared bell—
blue wisdom. *Say it,*

write it, speak it, chant it—sing
something—anything, beautiful or true.

THE OTHER VASTNESS

Had my father been twenty years younger I'm fairly sure
he would've dropped acid. I have no evidence for this,

except his adoration for the sound of Philip Glass.
How delighted I was sitting beside him at an intimate club gig,

orbiting side-by-side through inner space. Our conjoint flight
through spectrums of blue light: cornflower, teal, sapphire,

celeste, an indigo night sky. The closest we would ever come
to *dosing*. In high school he used to bust me regularly

for smoking weed in my upstairs bedroom then decently
stopped policing me once I'd left for university, allowing me

to regale old friends with a blown-glass rain-bowed bong—
that peace pipe of the suburbs. Nearing ninety, my father likes

to remind me that his time *is running out* while insistent he
can sense the universe expanding. Although he'll end this life

never having smoked a joint or ascended in cosmic time
to a god of rock guitar, we believe in music as the one true mode

that will help us go lightly towards the other vastness. Midway
through the concert I could see he was practicing. Reverie

crystallizing in his eyes as Glass played *Metamorphosis.* His visage
serene as if to say, *Yes—I am here, though I'll soon be elsewhere*

where words no longer matter, where our bodies will float
like astronauts weightlessly, endlessly among blue stars.

DONOR

I like to think of my kidneys in Dallas
and my liver in Atlanta. One lung in Portland
and one in Santa Fe. My heart where Tony
Bennett sang of his: at home in San Francisco.
What will be left then, nothing or spirit?
A heavenly ascent via cross of mountaintop
like Moses and Jesus?
                          I think what is holiest
is to leave everything here where I can from.
My jaw to a man who enjoyed a good smoke
as much as Freud or Groucho. My throat,
larynx, vocal cords and tongue to a father
who hums his flock of children off to sleep.

MY TINY MILES BIBLE

The gift in discerning how
to compose this life.

Trumpet buried in the ground.
Trumpet buried in the sky.

So What is the score
for timelessness in time.

But for here
there is no heaven.

IV. AT THE DOORS OF SLEEP BELOW THE TOWERS OF WAKING

The Going

i.
My sister swears by Ambien,
while milder insomniacs endorse Tylenol P.M.
ingested with an herbal blend of valerian root and chamomile.
Married male friends of mine (even those who sleep most nights
beside their wives) concur: internet pornography is best.

ii.
The sleepless are a regimen of ragtag soldiers
in combat with themselves. Counting debt, owls, losses,
barnacles, fiddler crabs and starfish, adding up piano keys
and harp strings, tallying the countless skulls draping Kali's neck.

I've known too many patients who wished to sleep forever
as they sat in psychotherapy.

I listened closely to their words,
which had they slept, would not have issued

from their lips:
compared with life, death's better.

iii.
There are few deeper
pleasures I know

than the journey
approaching sleep.

The forest and the darkness, in the forest
a deep well, the self in the dark going there,
becoming shadow, becoming lightness, then light, then dark,
becoming the deep well…

iv
Dr. Glass refers to it
as *sleeps' wondrous buffet.*
This lengthening abecedarian of tranquilizers and hypnotics:
Abilify, Cymbalta, Halcion, Lun-
esta, Sonata, Well-
butrin, Zo-
loft.

v.
Of my own home-remedies for inducing peace:

Remove the clear plastic cover from the clock face.
Extend index finger above the hour hand.
Rotate hour hand backwards, counter-clockwise over and over and over

until I'm a little boy again, wearing baseball pajamas with feet.
Get in bed wedged between father and mother.
Demand they read "The Red Balloon" then "The Velveteen Rabbit."

vi.
I listen to their voices
until I can't keep

my eyes
open

any longer.

Listen for a moment to wind's passing traffic.
Listen for a moment to whatever wind that is

wind.

vii.
Bliss when my body turns
into a place

and I remember everyone
I know and everyone

I don't know
are mutual pilgrims.

I carry the essentials:
Visas of breath and this

tiny lamp of sleep.
Although it's in the distance

it is light
enough to find my way.

APNEA

In the morning you report
how I frightened you

when I sporadically
stopped breathing.

How my ominous
stillness wakened you

in my nightly
near-death simulation.

I think the body almost
breathless

must be praying
for itself:

> *Shake me awake.*
> *Don't let me perish*
> *between dreams.*
>
> *Hold* me *wistfully*
> *as one about to place*
> *a summer violet*
>
> *in the middle*
> *of a hard-bound book*
> *to save it.*

DEAD LIGHT

Dark morning rain-dark morning,
day begins with dead light.

Along the hallway's length
two lines of scrolled newspapers eerily wait

for the sound of unlocking doors.
Morning rain-

dark morning, no means of escape
and nowhere to escape to.

The stairwell in the dream was
an Escher drawing.

It's far too early for the neighbors
to start quarreling

as bacon strips gurgle in pig fat
and oatmeal boils into

a geyser about to blow.
Dark morning

rain dark morning, another day
steeped in dead light.

Is it God, *dark morning,*
or only bone-weight gloom

that tethers us?
Black umbrellas tremble

on the street below
while house-trained dogs

frantic to urinate, paw
and whimper at their doors.

THE ORIGAMI OF WAKING

My two arms folded
across my chest:

a half-finished owl.

One arm resting along
your naked back:

the sleeping tulip.

The invention of paper,
although one hundred years

after the crucifixion,
shaped another renewal:

these other frames
in which we meet:

*two cranes alighted
in the jade-dark meadow.*

THE ATLAS OF LOST SLEEP

1. Insomnia's Birds

The pre-dawn birds chirp their pity. Sunrise
only brings death nearer.

Go back to bed and stay, until you figure out:
the why, the what, the where.

These singers can't be any clearer: *you you-*
you-you in curlicues, *you you-you you*

who've forgotten how to live—live scared.
Crack the window open for

a little air. The sidewalks, churchyard stones
have fallen end-to-end to form

a leaden river. The pre-dawn birds resume
tweeting high-pitched *pity.*

They can't be any clearer. One dawn
seagull lost inland, cries out

across the sky, understudy for
the song-less man.

2. Corpse Practice

He didn't know what else to do, but lay there staring at the ceiling.
He dubbed it, *corpse practice* or *what life would be like living like a mandarin*
I mean *a mannequin:* a smooth, featureless figurine lifted from Kostabi.

Some nights he'd try to force the hours to pass faster, drawing maps up-
on the bedroom air, then setting them ablaze inside his brain—singeing
some, charring others, compiling a hymnal of losses or envisaging

facelessness—his own or others: the melted eye-and-nose-less stares
of decorated soldiers scorched by roadside explosives, and the daughters
of Sharia law entering their schoolrooms, seared by automotive acid.

If only a few extravagant flowers had been dispatched to his nightstand vases,
he might actually believe, daylight means climbing from an open coffin.

3. Icarus as Flight Controller

In the hour before dawn, the insomniac aloft in his high-rise bed
assumes the role of flight controller:

to oversee the routes between LAX and JFK, the pigeon-clouds forming
around old women tossing breadcrumbs in the air, of plastic bags
wind-puffed into cavernous blossoms. And a last instruction, received telepathically:

Whenever in a holding pattern, remember
your mythic wings.

You are not you but a shadow of you, flying beneath the earth.

4. When Words Are My Only Sleeping Pills

Dawn, please do not come quickly.
Allow me to lay here an un-mined vein of silver hidden within myself.
Allow me to glow awhile in the dark, an iceberg unhinged from a grander body.
Grant me a nameless place, breathing between the two night-rivers.
Have the mourning begin without me, as it will for the wily baker, absolved
        in a cloud of flour.

LAZARUS

During the months of Bell's Palsy re-hab,
he was sent to various specialists
who would teach him how to teach himself what his body had forgotten.

He could smile with only one side of his mouth. One eye
refused to wink. Women thought
he was a pervert when he tried to flirt.

At the end of each session, his therapist handed him photocopies
of do-at-home exercises to help raise the upward curve
of the left half of his mouth and train his left eye

unrelentingly ajar, to drop like curtain
during sleep. He rarely practiced. No plaques, no trophies, no cash
prizes, no medals, not a carrot on a stick.

The complete banality of healing
is what he thought, unable to grasp why others clung
so avidly to yoga mats and weight-room gloves.

Unknowingly she taunted him with her pouty lips,
as she explained how "the tiny muscles and sensitive nerves
that surround the mouth would benefit from long, slow kissing."

If only he could summon the ample nerve
to entreat her to perform a feat of biblical proportion
and resuscitate the man he was.

V. NO HEROES

Biopsy

Her steady scalpel
shaves away
millimeters
of reactive flesh

for the diagnostic
lab to evaluate
if my cells are
injurious or well.

I'm instructed to
*call for the results
next week.* Either
cheerful news

or a preface to
more hair loss
and debilitating
queasiness. She's

removed a dot-
sized mole, odd-
brown punctuation
mark. I prefer

to think, my
dermatologist took
and in return,
gave nothing back.

When in fact
she bartered
this soft rind
for a scar.

MRI

The technician sought to make it pleasant.
He was chatty and exceedingly kind.

Though the device about to swallow me
bellowed like a horror-film monster;

its shape a reminder of the ancient
tombs I'd photographed while roving

through Cappadocia.
To put myself at ease I tried

to pretend the procedure was a ride
through *The Tunnel of Love*

like the one in fire-red gondola we'd hired
for an hour tour of the Venice canals.

Our bodies pressed close, gliding
varnished by the Dorsoduro light.

And how later, amidst the clusters
of loud tour groups,

we both stopped talking
and listened to the hour

bells and watched
the ageless horses galloping on air.

RECOVERY ROOM, LENOX HILL

I woke enclosed
by walls robin-
eggshell-blue, far
from earth and self,
never having known
such peace. Each lobe
finely stewed in
anesthetic gases.

Those in worse condition
must remain here
overnight, supine
or one-third upright
beside short-stemmed
flowers in inexpensive
vases and baskets of
exotic fruit. Nurses

crank the beds up
and down and down
and up. Patients
dressed in snow-
white gowns like
hermits who compose
haiku in forests and
on boats. Floating

deeper down than
sleep, a voice cried,
Gologatha, which
turned my being
gossamer, though
I'm sure to wreck
and ruin again in
spite of better health.
If only this vision
holds, even after

I've let go of this
IV-pole I cling to,
a watchman
to his lantern,
a shepherd to his crook.

LYME CONVALESCENCE

A single deer
tick

riveted and sunk
like a tiny flag into his flesh.

Debility at fifty wasn't
something he'd prepared for.

A teacher, suddenly unable to
read or write or speak.

The left half of his face
collapsed, flaccid

and dripping
like one of Dali's clocks.

With a glut of useless time
to pass, he'd gimp

his days through Central Park,
marveling and grieving

at the normal vigor
of un-afflicted bodies.

His image on the walkways
like a hollow stain or

a misshapen keyhole
belonging to a door
he felt compelled to
open and pass through

into a strangely vacant
room, where he'd remain
for an unspecific time,
awaiting new instructions.

Though occasionally,
he'd veer from the concrete paths

to stand among gargantuan
oaks, until their muscled

shadows cast him out again—
sutured, in sunlight.

THREE MOMENTS IN THE HISTORY OF BEING FED

At The Last Supper there was honey, figs and olive oil.
Whether the thirteen men ate lamb remains debated
though the coursing matters less than the truth that time betrays us.

Mother was too frail to order Peking duck or crab cakes
and even if she could've, it wouldn't have been scrumptious,
pureed to a gruel to prevent obstruction.

In her final weeks, what she mostly *swallowed* (for one
could hardly deem such mouth-work, "eating")
was applesauce baby-spooned from a cold Mott's jar.

I fed her with a gentle care just as she'd fed me
Hagen Daaz and Jell-O when I stayed home from
grammar school, recovering from a tonsillectomy.

NO OTHER SHELL

A woman of refinement, I'd have thought
she'd be revolted when severing their sautéed limbs.
But Mother savored soft-shell crabs in season and I liked
to watch her squeeze a firm half-lemon over them
in glistening drops, her self-satisfied stabs at the broccoli florets,
her effort to ignore the creamy pool of polenta, until
she surrendered, gulping down a few warm dollops.

Everyone we love will soon be torn apart.
The wishes in her will—specific: *cremation only*.
"Burn me to a crisp as if we lived along the Ganges,"
she once blurted out, after downing two carafes of French Chablis.

Amidst Stage IV as soft-shell season ended
she lost her palate for crustaceans: Shrimp Fra Diavolo,
linguine in white clam sauce. Sitting through
our leisurely, long familial meals like a weary child
twisting noodles around her fork. Paler by
the day, paler by the hour, and not for one moment
near the end was her body briefly golden.

THREE SHORT POEMS ABOUT ONE LUNG

I. Hair, Smoke and God

Summertime and mother's dying—not too fast, not too slow.
Seated at the dining table, she eyes the white matter of cauliflower,
her stony baked potato, the herb-roast wing and neck and makes-
believe (for family sake) she's really eating as she guides her unfilled
fork around the plate. Later, like a good Hassidic, she'll lie without
her treatment wig beside my father in the dark, insisting in whispers,
God as a concept is pathetic, though her mind's run out of options
whose to blame. And she can't precisely say what it was that did *this*,
aside from girlish stints with cigarettes and that brief despair that
came each dusk while her husband was at work, and she'd light
a Kent and sip a can of Miller with the promise of a *High Life*.

II. Stage IV: Tidy Up

Folding up her final months neatly as a Macy's blouse,
until the end she was domestic. She considered death
much tidier than life, delighted to flout Jewish law:
"only cremation is hygienic." Once her oncologist used
the term "Stage IV," she'd knew never see another off-
Broadway performance. Her favorite comment on
the treatment flops of life-long friends, "better gone
and sooner." Her children understood that she'd never
tolerate the vanities of aging: frowzy sorceress-white hair,
the indignities of a wheelchair or a walker. A life flanked
by a portable oxygen tank and a bored geriatric nurse,
killing listless hours on a bench in Central Park. Mother
always saw each dust-mote as a slow assault, knowing
our triturated earth is all she would become.

III. Too Many Rivers To Cross

We hear a crooning Jimmy Cliff as we stand out
on her terrace. "Sitting Here in Limbo" and other
reggae classics to ease our preparatory sorrows.
Tumid heat, the sundown glow, summer leaves
un-stirring in the late August air. He sings of *waiting
for the tide to turn,* and the benefits of ganja for those
who worship Jah and love to toke and dance. Mother
refuses all palliative care as her diet dwindles to *Ensure.*
We plead with her to try "just once," a caplet of
medical marijuana. Our dread is pure as we rub
her scraggy back—the loosed flesh drooping from her
collarbones like grisly curtains. We hold her close
as we hold our vigil. Cliff warbles, *it won't be long…*
This show will end without an encore.

PUB CRAWLS

In an hour long past midnight, we'd stroll away from the stately
habitations and sit in a non-descript Irish bar on Lex to conduct
a post-mortem on another bleak day. Though the house-wines
were screw-top dreck, my sister downed four half carafes of white
while I pounded Guinness pint by pint. What was there to recall
about those nights except that they were ghastly. Mother, a pallid
waste, gasping as she strained to suck the ever-thinning air.
Our family, like Himalayan mountaineers who'd come to realize
dying is also an ascent. When we brought her in for her decisive visit
to her nonchalant oncologist, we sensed his impatience—wasting
precious time on an invalid with a doom-and-gloom prognosis.
A journey those last weeks from impudence to apathy and surely no
more strength to reminisce. By then we'd reassessed what triumph is:
not fighting for an inert life but a savage giving-up and in. We both
admitted being tempted to taste her high-grade morphine, which
she hardly took, fearing madcap visions followed by an overdose,
but we didn't have the nerve and merely languished on our barstools,
discussing her brief verdicts and terse reviews of Broadway shows
and art-house films at Lincoln Plaza. "Awful," "stupid," "terrible,"
"I hated it." Lexicon fitted to a cancer death. And yet, regarding
her life journey, we never knew *her truth*—a specialist she was
in keeping secrets from herself. Whenever father left her bedside,
one of us would spoon her atop the wildly flowering duvet,
while the other sibling stood gazing blankly at the panoramic view
of remote control sailboats circling the pond, daydreaming
of those raucous sea lions gliding through the waters at the zoo.

A RIVER AS WE HAD BEEN TOLD

No boat docked nearby.
No boatman alongside the paint-chipped stern
waiting to ferry her across.

Not a paddle. Not a single oar.
Not one life preserver
the color of gaudy flames.

We were not surprised:
time was not a river anymore,
not a river as we had been told,
as we'd been led to believe all these years.

Neither buoyed, nor streaming,
neither floating nor flowing away.
No grace, not God's, nor anyone's. (Her oncologist
to prescribe enough morphine).

If there was a living and benevolent water,
it was not anywhere near to her.
Only blanched sand and a filament
of self—

translucent anchor sinking
from the visible
world.

There were signs that final week—thirst,
inexorable thirst, a ravenous thirst.
heartless in its magnitude.

Her jaw like a rusted gate
its hinges make hardly
creaking open.
The water glass, the tablespoon,
the plastic cup,
the gulping and the gulping
again.

*Drink... Good... Take
a sip... One more... Good...
good—*

that's it.

NOTES ON A COMPARATIVE MOURNING

"In taking these notes I am trusting myself to the banality that is in me.
Not to pray, to bless…Is it not to this mourning should lead." —Ronald Barthes

There are mornings so sad.
The waking mind in loss returns to loss.

Barthes rarely exploited metaphor in his discourse
on grief, though I concur when he wrote, *suffering is*
rust, mud deposited on the heart.

He revered his mother always and only in superlatives: *dignity,*
courage, energy, benevolence, nobility. Sweetness.

My mother while noble too was outspoken without mercy.
Her kindness interspersed with rage, her generosity
melded with hostility. She equipped me early

for enduring her displeasure, which led to banishments—
a childhood as catacomb, Etruscan tomb. Little exiles
without a bridge or ladder.

During her last decade, I moved back to New York.
We'd see each other weekly, and yet, over the telephone,
before hanging up, and despite re-confirmed plans to meet,
she'd invariably ask again, "when will I see you, sweetheart."

After those Upper Eastside trattoria suppers,
Mother liked to stroll Romanesque, locking arms. I never
overcame the Oedipal awkwardness of those languorous walks
along East 86th. Queasiness induced by a blend
of longing and repulsion. A feeling I couldn't transcend
until lying with her as I hadn't in forty years.
The two of us alone, while my father sobbed in the den.
Her deathbed that was their lover's bed until infirmity exhausted all desire.

Barthes in an index card entry on January 30th, 1979:
We don't forget but something vacant settles in us.
Our childlessness, which ended

105

when our aging mother's turned into our own first progeny.
I who had not procreated, I had in her very illness engendered my mother.

My mother was weak, very weak. I lived in her weakness.
It was impossible for me to participate in the world of strength,
to go out in the evenings, all social life appalled me.

Eventually, Barthes concedes to the triumph of Eros
over Thanatos: *The habits, flirtation, attraction, a whole*
discourse of desire, of I-love-you.

Sex the grand palliative.
The make-up sex, the sex before escaping, before vanishing,
before moving in with someone else.
The mercy-fuck to let you know I still find you sufficiently attractive,
still adequate in bed even though it's undeniably over.

A year after my mother's death she remains sonically audible
as if pre-recorded. How does her voice locate
within me with such precision without a body
or a mouth? Sordid ventriloquism? Cosmic joke?
How peculiar her voice, which I knew so well and no longer hear.

The rooms vacated by her absence still hold the afterglow
of her presence. Especially the leather chair her body occupied
as she sat with a novel, a crossword puzzle, gossiping on the cordless phone.

I pour a glass of Pinot Noir and sit in *her* chair
watching the sky dim above the tree line, in between
the darkening gate formed by the Dakota and San Remo.

Her dying: the only primal scene
I've ever witnessed. Their conjugal bed complete
with moaning and fluids dripping from every orifice.

Only a gnawing disturbance now when I look at Mother
in photo albums: embalmed in snapshots with that frozen smile,
the green rivers of her eyes devoured by time.
An older self-replaces a younger self over and over and over

till the last that is nothing—an image that is imageless. Her being here
when I was not here, and me now here without her.

And even one year later,
not even her recollected voice. *A localized*
deafness book-ended by non-being.

Without her in the rain, without her in windowed daylight,
without her in Central Park among the daffodils and jonquils.
Without her hands I'd watch impeccably place long-stemmed tulips
in her favorite glass vase. Her life undetectably
illuminating less and less of my life.

Only at the end did I notice
I'd become
a torch for her.

LOVE DUCK

My father, through his tears beseeches me to write a poem
about Mother and I going out for Chinese food without him.
Frankly, I'm suspicious. I think he wants to know what we
were doing in his absence. Did we dine face-to-face? Sit
side-by-side in a plush banquette? Did we toast with Mai Tai's?
Or lean mutually over as to sip from our Scorpion Bowl,
twirling tiny parasols and laughing? We're without him at
Shun Lee East where seasoning might induce anything
from a rash to a coma. Mother and I here in private
discussing the productions of Gurney and Mamet, the Johns'
retrospective, the new non-fiction by Tracey Kidder.
Her merciless opinion on installation art invading Chelsea.
I tried to convince her she shouldn't be concerned that
the Knicks starting five are swathed in seaweed-dark tattoos
as long as they're still winning. And not hastily dismiss
The Sopranos for their non-stop use of expletives. I'm sure
that my father was unworried about leaving me alone with her.
He'd seen me countless times shudder in my PF Flyers
and nearly pee my bell-bottoms jeans whenever he yelled
FUCK!!!! about my latest misdemeanor. In his anguish,
he want to feel that we were *close.* So I don't mention how
amidst our gastronomic pleasure, she couldn't help scorning
this, excoriating that, or how the copious libations pacified
those suppers, and the fact that she'd insist on paying.
I remind him only how his absences allowed us to celebrate
our lust for Beijing Duck: that crackling skin, the slightly
gamy meat, scallions crisp, the ooze of night-sky plum sauce,
pancakes warm and soft inside their lacquered dragon box.
It was divine inside: the doting staff in bow ties, the grease-
less spring rolls, the dumplings erotic with their aromatic
broth inside. Perfection amidst a shared ambivalence we'd
never fully overcome. We'd start with bone-in spare ribs.
Like a caveman, I'd gnaw into the marrow, and much to her
annoyance. All the while noticing couples, middle-aged
and older at other tables, who'd occasionally glance at us,
and might've thought, perhaps with envy, perhaps with
pleasure: *here sits a son and mother who purely adore each other.*

VI. THE LAST WORLD

Between Blood Rivers
After Lorca

Vendors peddle sugarcoated nuts—false bronze glinting
behind warmed glass. After strafing rains, you'll find
cut-rate umbrellas shoved into trashcans, dead wings
like derelict sails flapping against the chain linked fences.

New York, mire, New York, wire and death. Every day they
slaughter four million ducks, five million hogs, two million pigeons.
At the uptown matinee, sit among the Jewish widows
then walk west where the abattoirs were dislodged

by rows of chic boutiques, their parquet floors without
a tinge of steakhouse blood. Consider all those
idle men, kin to former priests who donned snowy aprons
splattered with an honest gore. Loiter

in the semen-white dawn outside a padlocked church
as an ambulance shrieks past like cats in heat.
Or stand beneath an elevator of shimmering glass
and follow the upright coffins as they plummet from the cloud-

banks then rise against the sun. After midnight
saxophones, you'll hear with pristine clarity
the syncopated droplets from a *tepid faucet* break apart
and *the awakened earth cast off trembling rivers of moths.*

SUBTERRANEAN

I. The Horizontal Fires

Level by level I descend
        to the sound of clanging metal.
                Steel doors open and I enter
                        and ride what seems like hours
                                in a landscape without weather.

No guide except a map enclosed
        in glass like a transparent body
                from *Gray's Anatomy,* rivulets
                        of arteries and veins. The signal
                                on my cell phone to the world

above gone dead. I walk from car
        to car to gaze upon this afterlife
                they've led—chained to metal poles
                        and handrails and left to beg.

One car of upright sleepers
        seems at peace until I witness
                how they're shocked awake
                        once-a-minute, as nightmares
                                passed from brain to brain.

In a car smeared with graffiti
        the inhabitants are mostly poets and
                their critics who mutter to themselves
                        while everyone else reads a matching newspaper
                                with a front page photo of a skyscraper frozen.

and the headline: **ARMAGEDDON!**
        I continue forward secretly protected.
                Biggie's ghost infusing me with hip-hop
                        swagger. When I reach the front car—
                                it's apparent—the train has no conductor,

so I climb into the driver's vacant chair where
    I behold a bright metropolis modeled upon heaven,
        this chariot surging in between the dual necklines of
           the bridge strung with arcs of pearls. Relentless wheels
               in their course, sparking above the ice-chunked river.

II: Toward the Natural History

Three sisters sitting side-by-side-by-side well groomed for Sunday church.
I wonder where their mother is?
Each girl is flaxen-blonde, wears patent leather shoes
that glint like those in Oz. Each one is playing parent with a doll:
one doll dressed in overalls ready for a square dance. A lithesome
plastic ballerina encircled by a pink tutu posed in a pleat.
Barbie in war fatigues outfitted for a tour of duty in Baghdad
or Kabul. With peach-and-cream complexions, these girl appear
as though they're headed to an *Ivory Soap* commercial.

A man in the adjoining seat wheezes repetitiously—
it sounds as though its chronic emphysema.
He whispers, "you—
be careful," in my ear.
I have no choice except to listen.
I certainly won't look at him or query for elaboration.
Is he a vigilante or insane or just another harmless recluse
seeking liberation in the fetid air?

One stop past Columbus Circle, the sisters vanished.
I didn't see them rise and leave as the car filled up with Yankee's caps
and bundled strollers. Only two more stops
until the Planetarium. *Should I stand and walk*
into another car? Be still, I tell myself,
maintain your focus while glancing at the strip ads
for STANLEY KAPLAN courses, the GED in Spanish,
institutes for long-haul truckers and future cosmetologists.
His bulk presses in on me.
His halitosis makes me gag.
His bulbous head reminds me of Serrano ham with eyes.
I watch his cosmic gaze transfixed on nothing I can see,
unless his occupation is conversing with the dead.

III. In the Church of Fading Voltage

Gazing down the platform at 5ᵗʰ and 53ʳᵈ the tunnel lights illuminate
each nook and niche where wooden saints will stand with missing hands
and severed heads. Deserted shrines where candles burn upside-down

and disembodied prayers are hollowed out by grinding metal.
Now the sole inhabitants are monk-brown rodents, scurrying to sermons
across the grease-black rails within the church of fading voltage.

A train arrives. I hide my face behind the gossip pages of the *Post*.
I stand beside a man with a giant sequined crucifix
suspended from his neck and ferret furred along his shoulder.
We surge past midnight platforms nearly empty except for crumpled pages
of Tuesday's *Wall Street Journal* and Metro Cards without a ride left.
Inside these jangled cars above 125ᵗʰ, clowns and necromancers suddenly appear,

nomadic healers hawking pelts and claws, tortoise shells, teeth and glands
in vials. "TB, Ebola, HIV, which is your disease?" A sickly child asks,
tugging at my sleeve. "You'll really need those Gucci loafers even

when you're dead?" Lead me out from where I am, Beatrice from Riverdale,
Hermes from Canarsie. Extract these jittered nerves; forge these dreaded wheels
into enduring stars. And upon this rusted nail hang a dawn-light lantern.

iv. Underground Music

Guitarists from Argentina, Cuba and the Cameroon, instruments
with just one string
                              that twangs and weeps, evokes
past loves
                                        to chill the blood.

A Brooklynite blows Charlie Parker.
                              Two couples in embroidered vests
                                        dance a Polish polka.

I have nowhere I must be, no pressing
destination.

Another hapless Orpheus
entranced by the current of her scent.

She's reading a Balzac paperback
with a Degas bather on the cover
as if we'd met in a long ago lost hour.

Black cowboy boots, a floppy red felt hat,
a guitar case strapped to her back.

Her mast, I think.
In a moment, she'll sail off
on my pilfered breath.

One drummer from Burundi, another
one from Senegal.
Peruvians with wooden flutes
summoning macaws from rain-soaked jungles.

Other phyla soon arrive:
a barbershop quartet of rats, and a frazzled artist
whose moniker is *Cockroach,*
his carapace a French beret.

A stout fellow in an alpine suit
taps his boot to cold cement
as he swoons with his accordion.

A white-gloved Michael Jackson clone
with a troupe of break dance acrobats
wind a path in between
the "Wet Paint" columns.

I wish I could follow her and not look back.
Find myself reborn inside
her Cobble Hill apartment,
the music of old plumbing as we ran the bath.

It's grace that haunts me as I wait
never having learned to flow,
except in some pen-push rage at the solitary desk.

This task seems all too arduous:
become
an original on the surface.

Like others here I fled and went below
to strum and croon and bop
for a moment's admiration
and a guitar case strewn with dollars.

Gaunt hipsters and grizzled folkies stand beneath these filthy L train stairs
to serenade Kurt Cobain, John Lennon,
and Joe Strummer.

Earthly life is Hell's disguise
for those who chose this realm instead.
No skinhead metal,
no gangsta' beats,
no nihilistic grooves. Only
harp and gamelan, dulcimer and didgeridoo.

BLACK OUT

A lone bodega lit by propane lamp,
peddling expired milk and overripe bananas.

Not one proprietor willing to unlock their barroom
for us to drink ourselves into a bright oblivion.

This must be the end, we thought
but didn't say.

Our flashlight beams like dislocated eyes
mystified by the impassable dark.

Along the blacked-out streets
we crafted a private apocalypse:

Dead stoplight overhead
creaking like Diogenes's lantern.

No sirens, no car alarms, no howls, no pleas,
no murmured prayers.

Not even the scratch or squeak of vermin—
our islands' rightful sovereigns.

We walked guardedly among vacated buildings,
convinced an amorphous beast

was skulking around corners,
trailing its prey with frothing tongues.

BLACK LIGHT FOR ETHERIDGE KNIGHT
after Terrance Hayes

Count those living a locked-up life who sleep with one-
eye open, always open. Black is the horse running from
the fires. *Ka-toum Ka-toum, Ka-toum. Ka-toum.* Black are
the horses galloping in silhouette across the stone-white
face of the moon. This song in which the dream-god said,
I will give you two hands that cut with the skill of Kara Walker.
The dead you left behind on Korean fields. The near dead
you lived among in wintertime on Midwestern city streets.
Those kept temporarily warm by Pluto's snowy-light.
The cemeteries of the heart one carries like an ancient vision.
Who among us is not less than their history of grief?
Who's never drowned in the wine of their own blood?
Who's not been beset with a vision of America without
its prisons, shelters, slums? I too lost faith in the systems;
sustained only by friendship, family, forgiveness, art. How
you sung the talking drum, the kindness drum. Bearded bard
of Memphis, Indianapolis, Pittsburgh. King of cobalt. King
of indigo. *Ka-toum. Ka-toum, Ka-toum.* Ever-shadowed by
a racial blues: its horses, her tender hands. That primordial
blue where the stars still yearn to feel themselves scatter.

WINTER CITY LULLABY

Trashcans in the alleyways flame like orphaned stars.
Cold drums silvered with midnight's frost. Sleepily
I walk the dim Chinatown streets, littered with stumps
of leeks and carrots and a scattering of bean sprouts
that guide me past a peep shows' ruby neon to a chain-
linked parking lot, where drab repetitious lights emit
a hollow glow. Several blocks beyond, beside a half-lit
office tower, one man plucks a warped guitar, another
finger-picks a banjo. A bearded gent with weather-beaten
hands pounds hard on some bongos. *Here and lonely
with the winter blues. I haven't got a lover and I haven't
got good shoes.* This band of soot-sad men harmonizing
as they stare into the glowing of yellow-blue arpeggios
while shreds of flame-tinged newsprint float midair.

SUBWAY: 3AM
"...sealed by the ghosts I do not know. Draw in your head and sleep the long way home."
—Hart Crane *Voyages*

She sat directly across from me.
I didn't resist furtively observing her.

Her shaking, her twitching—arrhythmic—
the nervous systems avant-garde percussion.

I tried to overhear what she was saying
to the empty space

as she muttered—hoarsely, guttural, barely
audible.

                    *

How the self interrupts the self. How the self—
interrupts. I'd been musing about desire:
New York women gossamer in cotton summer dresses,
baseball on the radio, cold gelato scooped from metal tubs.

You entered the Queens-bound A-train
with your catapulted heart, your brain screeching
like a terrified choir.

The first thing I noticed was your pro-football jacket
with the insignia of the Kansas City Chiefs.
I figured you must've come from there—the country of Dull Knife
and Drowning Bear. Your modest mid-western city
where your father might have heard Ben Webster, Joe Turner, Lester Young.

                    *

Most of the ride I pretended
to read The Daily News
                              while watching your head
fall left
        then right then
left again.

117

Your tired, tired head
                    in crooked-neck sleep
tilting like a metronome between your bony shoulder.

                    *

I made it home with a Corona tallboy and pint of Ben & Jerry's.
"My Heart Stood Still" on the radio
transmitted from Newark

I heard myself too, barely audible
as I wondered if anyone had woken you
once you reached the final stop in Far Rockaway.

Or if you were already Manhattan-bound again,
crossing above the coal-dark river
towards the vast electrified maze of monoliths.

                    *

After Billie Holiday finished "Strange
Fruit" I turned the sound off
and shut the lights.

I heard myself saying to the empty air:
*Sleep gently. Sleep
deep.* Then I asked

whatever spirits protect the night trains,
that you waken safe, and somehow less alone
in the wounded light I'd rather see, as *dawn.*

RIDING THESE DISRUPTED LINES:
THREE NEW YORK CITY SUICIDE ELEGIES
"…got static in my head, the reflected sound of everything,
Tried to go to where it led, but it didn't lead to anything," —Elliot Smith

1. Elliot Smith

The night has been re-routed. Lights of colored circles without order
as if inside a discothèque, an inscrutable, jumbled alphabet. A uniformed EMT
tinkers with his Blackberry, two straw-haired hipsters scrutinize a subway map
in Japanese, a jazz bass in its coffin with monocycle wheel,
held steady by a gray-beard cat with black Kangol beret. It's after 3 A.M.

The frat-house boys are shit-faced drunk on *Rolling Rock* and *Makers Mark,*
while young Hispanic dishwashers look exhausted, leaning
with their eyes closed, on one another's shoulders. The headlines are in Spanish.
I read the word *Iraq* and *muerte* denotes dead. On the radio this morning
I heard the doleful music of another wordsmith overdosed. *Whichever*
train I take tonight, I'll ride beside his restless ghost. We strain our ears to grasp

the MTA's instructions. The voice over the loudspeaker is garbled beyond
comprehension. We might as well be underwater. The platform has become
a gangplank in my mind. Most passengers appear resigned and calmly numb.
A homeless man turns a rancid jacket into a blanket. Two scholars wearing yarmulkes
sit debating Talmud. While all the artists waiting here nod their heads repeatedly
as if before the Wailing Wall, wired to their I-Pods, singing with the singing dead.

II. Spaulding Gray

A small moon quivers above the Hudson River as it did above the Yangtze
thirteen hundred years ago when poets understood their lives were nothing

less or more than leaves adrift and falling blossoms. I think of
Spaulding Gray on the Staten Island ferry, staring at the wallet-photos

of his wife and toddler son, showing them to passengers nearby,
who'd become unwitting rowers on his Styx.
                                        Tonight at a local trattoria
I sip a vintage Nebbiolo. I sink my nose into the crystal and inhale.

A perfect moment, almost…
The injured mind unravels and the blankness in its wake
scourges courage, hope and love.

You always struck me as approachable,
though I'm certain had I passed you on a Sag Harbor sidewalk
      or dining at a nearby table,

             I'd have uttered nothing.

Taciturn and star-struck,
I'd seen all of your films and monologues off-Broadway.

III. Liam Rector

I never purchased any of your books or borrowed a single volume from a library
or friend. I'm not embarrassed. North America is backlogged with *must-read* poets.

Regardless, I'd long admired the title of your first collection and would have stolen it
if I could. *"The Architecture of Sorrow,"* I always thought it brilliant. When I lived

two years depressed in Cambridge, we attended the same readings. Several evenings
we sat drinking at the same alehouse booth or mint tea table. A few esteemed bards,

along with other younger, tag-along and (like myself, destined to become) lesser poets.
You consistently ignored me, though I really didn't mind. Rivard and Sleigh were

always nicer. I admit I had no interest and didn't follow your career. I knew you taught
at Bennington, but by then I'd lost all zeal for paying thousands for an older poet's praises.

For twenty years I skimmed your poems in journals. I even think, we published once
or twice in the same issues. The next thing I read of you was thoroughly impressive,

caddy-corner from the weather: one-eighth of a page in the New York Times devoted
to your work and death. Cancer followed by suicide is not without some logic. Though

I wasn't so much shocked that you'd died, for one could do far worse than sixty-five,
but surprised how all these years we lived in the same neighborhood, merely blocks away.

AT A URINAL IN THE WHITE HORSE TAVERN

After one more pint of Harp, I'll teeter out alone,
replenished by the February air and long cold rows
of bodega flowers that glow beyond midnight
like a funerary altar. *Over the past table I repeat this
present grace.* Although my own words only perish
in their moment. I drank for several hours
with my back to your drab portrait, recalling songs
of *broken ghosts with glow-worms, the slash of vision.*
No coroner never testified if diabetes or cirrhosis
eventually unmoored: *A black reward for a roaring life.*
I too never found the will to find a *wiser mirror.*

BEST IN SHOW

Whenever I'm in earshot of any well-bred owner
I wonder if, in some prior life we weren't all
once coddled hounds or wouldn't wish to be. Or better
yet, a poodle groomed into decorative shrubbery
at home in his duplex overlooking Central Park.

Most dogs around the globe are underfed
and roam unpaved roads in crazed voracious packs.
Mutts that hop three-legged or shield a mangled paw
as they limp amongst their cronies fixed in
tantric poses, trying to evict incessant broods of fleas.

How strange to walk Tribeca streets amidst
these privileged pets, to overhear their
renowned names as their master's lavish
praises. Good boy, *Orwell Mingus Bartok
Kissinger Thoreau.*

HAIKU CITY

What brings sidewalk mirth?
One man with seven leashes:
Bichons, Pugs, Shih Tzus.

In Grand Central Station
overhead stars dark-teal sky
as real as real sky

The Highline is not
that high. Too many fake monks
looking for money.

After the parade
Charlie Brown like Spiderman
dragged off, deflated.

On the MET roof I
fall in love with our skyline
over and over.

Chinatown windows:
100 ducks nose-diving—
roasted yellow-gold.

Another Knicks loss:
loyal fans, heads bowed file
out of the Garden.

Many nights I've been
spared ravenousness by two
slices and a Coke,

The Empire State
Building lit up like the mind,
delighting the night.

On beds of crushed ice
shrimp that haven't lost their heads:
eyes black as raindrops.

After dying down-
town, Lou on the radio
still crooning *Sweet Jane.*

Tony Soprano
Batman Capote—the last
act the same for all.

Turrell-made sky, I'm
supine in the Guggenheim
breathing holy light.

Late-night hunger in
K-town: ban chan BBQ
stone bowl Bi Bim Bop.

Certain that no one
is looking, the carousel
horses close their eyes.

Unable to sleep
the cockroach and I begin
to pray for daybreak.

GRAY STONES ON GRAY STONES
after Vallejo

   I will die in New York City amidst ashen flurries.
A moment I already remember.
I will die in New York a forgotten effigy who abandoned his own voice.
On an unseasonable Monday as it is today, in a windy November.

   It will be Monday, because today, Monday, as I prose
these lines, the long bone which dovetails my shoulder
is a clock that measures out each second, a scrawny cane,
which enables me to turn to see myself alone.

   Peter Marcus has died; they bumped into him on sidewalks
without apology, all of them, everyone, though he's done
nothing to them; they gave it to him with briefcase, heel and elbow

   likewise with designer handbags, the leashes of their dogs;
witnesses are the Mondays and my weakened labrum
this separateness, the wet sky, the avenue unending.

THE NORTHERN HOURS

I. COLD

Little Vortex

Standing beside a surging brook I prefer a mobile paradise.
I have no interest in stiller waters: pools and ponds where
     others noticed long ago a splendor that mirrors the sky.

I will shun the lakes in Westmore and Barton and follow
the green candle of each pine as their wicks are ignited by
the rising sun until a little vortex calls me as Echo did sighing

to Narcissus and let the currents spin me in a blindfold
of longing till I can't ascertain if I'm going towards or away
from myself, into the future or the past. I will kneel there,

rinse my eyes, remembering those losses that did not end
with vision then wander off in search of an image one might love.
I will sleep on the firm floors of the late-autumn orchards

where the pears are labeled *Flemish Beauties* and the apples,
Honeygold and pray to have some benevolent tenderness kindled
within me. And when the next sunrise comes I will listen for

a distant creek or brook, hoping I'll be returned to a sunlit river
where I wait for another little vortex to appear, a whirl that will
enable me to plainly see how everything and nothing reflects me.

WORDS AT DUSK

The words I lost at dusk:
amulet, totem. If only to defy
the onslaught of the rust.

The aging of the airtight
mind. The verses made
of dust.

Tomorrow is for
what? The autumnal sun
sinks beyond the stables

and the barns. The pasture
suddenly dimmer as if lit
by antique chandeliers.

AUTUMN MILKWEED

I saw the inner silks of their bodies.
Tufts loosened, unraveled by touch.
I remember how it was with us:
the soul conceived as fabric,
a weave that enabled the world
to sift through like gauze or
cheesecloth. I remember too
how in winter we came crunching
over hardened snow to inspect
the empty pods, imagining
the vanished fur had been pilfered
by angels and made into garments
for their wings

WILD TURKEYS

Wild turkeys
aren't noticeably
wild. They
loiter soporific
in the roadside
grasses. Wizened,
bored and with-
out recourse
to stick their
necks out.
World-weary,
their Egyptian
heads droop as
if their wattles
conceived
in mourning
were filled
with lead.

BLACK OAK

When the hand of each green leaf grabs me
simultaneously, by arms, wrists and shoulders,
the earth is not asking, where are you going? But,
why are you still here? Their muscular branches
seizing me as they did inside the madhouse, forceful
yet kind, in a time when I believed I was the last
interpreter of clouds. Tonight the black oak needn't
state the apparent: you exist in a life of pointless motion
with your gyroscopic heart that has never learned to nest
inside love. Glancing at my loosely tied boots, I see
they are the offspring of logs, the rain-ruined leather
like scaly bark. Though manufactured shoes as history
observes, are amassed alongside shorn women's hair
then stored inside extermination stockrooms, and
reminds me why I'm frightened of the primal shapes
of roots that plunge savagely downwards as if to
asphyxiate the earth. Looking up, between the solder
of branches at the multiple stars, I am close now as
pinwheels are to the lips of children whooshing them
in motion. I do not want to ponder how even one
brief glimpse of the shine of the cosmos requires
light years, and the stars like glinting fishhooks will
wait an eternity for each wretched, singing mouth.

FROZEN HOURGLASS

The clear fangs below the gutters
glistening with sunlight, refuse to
let go, even as they thaw.

I stand looking out from an upstairs
window, watching icy droplets fall
as if from a frozen hourglass.

Water, not sand measures passing time.
Wet footsteps invisible as death
chiming on the slate path to my door.

THIS YELLOW GENEROSITY

Easy to have lost track
of the last time
I saw the un-obscured sun

and felt the warmth of daylight
on my uncovered skin.

Your yellow generosity
seeping inside me.

> On this rare February morning
> I have no motive to debate whether you're
> a kindly god or a desolate star.

A NIGHT WALK IN THE COUNTRYSIDE TOWARDS THE NATIVITY

Through the slog of winter, one light remains on
inside the henhouse, blazing with the redolent glow

of Caravaggio's *Adoration*. Crisscross rural roads
nearly empty in the afternoon twilight. Each ranch house

beginning its private descent under the old quilts of snow.
Atop a distant ridge, a cell tower blinks blood red,

while eggs drop inaudibly into upturned crowns of straw.
I hear sheep and horses fuss and stir in roadside barns

and couples back to back as they toss and turn behind
their bedroom doors. Too many here that no longer

recall the last time they made love. In the countryside,
how many conceivable mangers? How many hearts wishing

to be re-born in the light of the body beside them?
Roads as empty as outspread darkness. The wood-

smoke scented with frankincense and myrrh. Prayers
heard only in the spaces between the stars.

FOR BEARING

The cattle in the hills are motionless before dusk
as if a great grief has beset them. They sound
inconsolable—wailing like the tenor during *Che
gelida manina.* I'm starting to suspect I haven't
grieved enough either, that I should try to
mourn daily, turn grief into a pro-active habit
like making the bed and flossing. Some cattle
are the colors of tombstones—Michelangelo's
marble quarried in Carrera and shaped into
the Pieta. Sometimes I feel the air aglow as it
hovers in aura above his dead body, then think
of her, of that holy feeling: the heft of mortal
sorrow as it sinks into her meaningless arms.

TO HELP ENDURE THE WINTER HE READS A FEW
TRANSTRÖMER POEMS EACH MORNING

Before going out to the driveway to his difficult-to-start-up-
beater of a Ford, when not running late
for work, he might pause and notice new deer tracks
in the snow—a fairy tale-like path
he would follow beyond the length of his front yard,
had he non-clock time.
                              And while scraping off
the overnight ice from the windshield, he might
conceive of those tracks as the unclasped necklace of pearls
like those his grandmother wore, then his mother, then
his sister. And remember
                              that he'd watched each one
put them on. Their similarly thin arms like wings
curved behind their necks. A single, solitary line of hoof prints
extending beyond vision. A necklace composed
of small, aligned planets—both imaginably
endless, passed forward without knowing by the dead.

ON A MID-WINTER MORNING BEFORE STACKING WOOD

I didn't want to go into the iron cold
while it was still dark out. Instead I stayed
in bed; half-awake and turned the volume up
on the radio to louden the news from Aleppo.

It is said there are oil-black angels and spirits
gossamer as moonlight. Why bomb hospitals
already without power, medicines, sutures or gauze
to stanch the bleeding? Why bomb city schools

where no children have attended for years
and the teachers live as refugees.
Not one correspondent guarantees
that help is on the way, nor promises more harm

won't be heaped on more harm. Another morning
when reading poems feels deficient. Instead
I keenly listen for hopeful phrases, hopeful words
like *peace talks,* like *ceasefire,* like *potable water.*

Newly cut cord-wood is unusually heavy; a greenish
tint runs along the core. Its antiseptic scent a mix
of peroxide and vinegar, such that someone desperate
enough might consider using it to sanitize a wound.

THE BURDEN
After Chesterton

In a wood-fenced field in Monahan I saw Christ's donkey.
He looked dead-tired having hobbled from Jerusalem alone.

Cloaked in nothing more than a shawl of morning rain.
He carried nothing on his back but the epochs. As I passed

I asked if he remembered being heart to heart with God.
He looked down, embarrassed, went back to chomping sod.

WHEN SNOW STARTS FALLING I FALL SILENT

A white cascade appears

       out
       of

   nowhere

```
  *       *
   *  *       *      *
*        *  *     *
   *   *     *         *
              *
     *     *       *
  *     *     *
                *
           *
```

How is it one arrives,
anywhere?

Seemingly from nowhere—
Seemingly from nothing—

with speed
surpassing light—.

From before here
to after there

no device has
yet to calculate.

No poet or meteor-
ologist will say.

THE SCARF

I want you close as a winter scarf
wrapped around my neck

midway between mind and heart
and warming both.

I want to be encircled
three times or at least twice,

with no room for icy
winds to sting the skin.

I adore your varied guises:
merino, cashmere and angora.

The wool blood red like love
broken open. The green of

our dense forest where I lost
you and search for you again.

GLOSSARY OF FLURRIES

Choreographies that
gradually bury.

Provisional spaces
for sudden dreaming.

Goodbye notes hastily
left unfinished by

the dead. Kin to *Bellium,*
Erigeron

and other minuscule

daisies. Silence I am
still a part of.

II. SMALL MYTHOLOGIES

Pastoral

With animals he lived in the carnal light. Pigs
in the open mating unperturbed,
the prolonged rueful ecstasies of doves
echoing through the woods, an ivory-faced goat
roped to a birch, two libidinous roosters
striding the wire coop. Every day a balancing

between the world of the body and the body
of the world. Clover crowns, yellow warblers,
loosestrife, primrose. Ducking beneath the clothesline
he'd walk through the orchard and sit below
the webbing of boughs. Jot in a notebook. Nap

on warm granite stones. Often he'd bring
a spoiled apple back inside the house, keeping
the scent on his fingers as he traveled
on the narrow roads of sleep. At dusk, he'd settle
in a yellow chair, its one stunted leg
tilting him like a passenger in an un-helmed boat.

From chilled morning silver till the burnt
fruit of twilight, he'd notice how his mind mated
and unmated words. Chipped teacup, moist
bread crumbs, the silence omnivorous and blue
as shadows cross the hills of crickets waking.

YARD SALES

The long folding tables on the front lawn stand empty.
No dreary blender or dish rack for sale, not a scrap
of glassware: ashtray, candy dish, no antique bottles
in celadon, mauve or azure to place on the kitchen sill
for amassing sunlight. No dream catchers or baseball
gloves. Not one bookcase or Big Wheels waits tagged
or labeled. All I'm really in the market for is a derelict
birdhouse and a large clawed hammer.
                                        Up ahead, I notice a row
of vehicles double-parked, so I think I must've come
to the wrong address and head back to my car. It turns out
the other yard sale isn't any better: a set of tent stakes
for the next Prometheus, a gas lantern auto-graphed by
Psyche, a collection of dead butterflies pinned on plywood—
reminder to its buyer of our soul's once buoyant travels.

DISPATCH FROM THE NORTHEAST KINGDOM

An eccentric village, I sensed it when I entered.
Each roadside mailbox sported a bantam rack
of antlers and burly men—their heads bowed
beneath the hoods of Chevy's, all wore beards
lengthier than those of Muslim clerics. I noticed
how nobody discarded broken appliances or
their toddlers' rusted tricycles even after they'd
outgrown them. And whenever I asked a local
to ask for *the time*, he'd coolly point—directing
my attention to the frenzied spin of the huge
serrated blade splitting long boards at the sawmill.
Every porch retained at least two rocking chairs,
amiably perched side by side and occupied by
retired ghosts, while the actual tenants inside,
persist on food stamps, subsidized heat, X-box,
Bud and weed. For half the year the snow falls
swift and boundlessly as in fairy tales and plastic
globes, cloaking the landscape in a pure peace
for miles. The rare glass windows unburdened
by opaque plastic had frosted into opalescent
mirrors reflecting the luster of stove-warmed
souls while smoke unfurled from every crowned
chimney, offering the skies an ashen flower.

APPLE SONG

Inside Rogers Orchard Farmstore
a poster on the back wall:

The Uses of Apples

extolling the choicest types for strudel
and baking, the virtue of the apple

as a natural toothbrush, an asset
in digestion. In autumn, I warm up

with a cup of mulled cider and if no one
else is around I close my eyes and

inhale the odor of renewal. I want to
possess them by name and color.

Indared, Mitsu, Cortland, Red
Delicious, Granny Smith, to praise

the role of the apple in knowledge
and longing, gravity and archery

in the still life's of Vuillard
and Cezanne. Apples chopped and mixed

with walnuts, nutmeg, and honey
for this day when oppression is memory.

SNOW ORCHARD

Garlanded in fur-trimmed hoods I couldn't see their faces
as they toiled with hoe and shovel, digging furrows beneath
the glazed snow crust. Although their speech was audible
from the roadside where I stood, I sensed their words
had come from faraway as those in dreams and picture books
I was read to as a child. They labored nearly breathlessly
as if snow was softer agate one could sculpt.

                          After setting down
their tools against the frozen trunks they reached into burlap
sacks, removing what appeared to be bulbs, though porous,
spongier—susceptible to indentation. Some coopery, others
bronze. I surmised they were planting the ova of angels
beneath the winter apple trees.

                      Once they'd finished, they left
in silence beneath the gibbous moon. I slipped through the wire
fence and walked among the furrows where the old apples kept
their fetid sweetness. Twilight winds swirling around as I listened
for any stirrings from the numb, gestating cherubs, those soon
to waken in a squall of drifting blossoms, in a whiteness they
will gather in late springtime, to dress their perfect nakedness.

FRESH EGGS

I've passed this sign a thousand times five days a week for the past ten years.
A hard right off 202 North then down a steep quarter-mile driveway
bordered by Lodgepole Pines.

The sign always disturbed me with its matter-of-factness.
Two stark monosyllables:

Fresh Eggs.

Not exactly a neighborly welcome or a well-designed enticement.
Fresh Eggs painted
in a shabby brownish-red on beige plywood.

One might think if these egg-sellers were really urgent for business
their sign might read: Free Range
                                Organic

Or: Delicious Eggs
                    8-6
            Localvore's Unite!

For shouldn't we be taking "fresh" for granted?
And who in their right mind would segue down a shadowy dirt track
for the sake of a dozen eggs?

This vendor never bothering to create a simple logo
or employ some basic graphic design that might compel
would-be buyers to veer from where they're headed.

My suspicion is these people aren't selling eggs
but harvesting human embryos for cloning stem-cells;
that once one reaches the bottom of the hill

there are no coops, but rather mobile homes
equipped for rapid surgeries.
Should an unsuspecting buyer

be male, he'll find himself hours later
waking from deep sedation
with new scars above where his kidney was.

God forbid, the shopper is a woman under forty-two
she'll be held with the roosters for a month
while under-going hyper-ovarian stimulation.

Once I turned into their drive and started to make my way down-
hill between the pines. I could see a cluster of trailers,
one rickety barn, and the steel-blue waters of the Quabbin—

the crossroads that once divided farms on the bottom.
I rolled down my window to listen. The wind yowled like Nipmuc
burial songs, their blood-beat drums and drowning voices.

UNINHABITED CABINS

Far back in the woods log cabins are four legged creatures
sinking through the layers of pine needles, moss and mud.
Their facades like those of weight lifters with strained looks
on their faces as they squat, grip, then heave ponderous
barbells overheard.
                    Long deserted, they consider *homo sapiens*
trespassers—a damaged species who cannot endure without
signs or names. Only rays of sunlight are welcomed in as guests
and the full moons' light that spreads a crisp white sheet
across the sagging floorboards for the dreamers dreaming
elsewhere.

CLOCK TOWER CROW

flat roof of the village clock tower
he assumes his lawful place
on a pedestal in the sky.

Perched there, all he does is nod
and swivel his svelte head,
repeating his private call to prayer—

a garrulous *ha-ha ha-ha.*
What's the joke? Time
itself of which the crow

as prince of nihilists
is utterly unconcerned.
Ha-ha… ha-ha—it's all absurd:

this small-town life
with hair salon, drive-through bank,
Chinese takeout, two bars,

two hardware stores,
the surrounding hills dotted
with apocalyptic churches.

Ha… ha-ha… ha… ha…
We know you as you are:
time's onyx wing—

wing that spare our sight
from the other
coming darkness.

The Inaccurate Sign

warned:
BEWARE OF DOG
when it's men
whom we should dread,

those
who unleash them.

WOODPECKER TIME

I.
The Pileated woodpeckers hard-hollow knockings
on the borders of the summer meadow indicate
the hurry they're in to complete a good day's work.

With dusk sieving through the treetops, and crickets
ringing their jamboree bells, the woodpeckers fly above
the scraggy back roads to deliver their finished caskets

to the rustic hamlets, where grim morticians
wring their hands, envisioning ripe apples falling
with the snow. Boxes of varying lengths and widths strictly

measured to actuarial specifics. I want to ask *if*
I'm a recipient of one of their newest models or at least
be kept abreast of my number on their waiting-list.

I watch as the twilight enlarges space, and what seemed
Near appears as indelibly far: sawmill dust, tin roof rust,
the lungs of toppled chimneys. I can see from this

distance: a copse of birches kneels to gather up
their shadows. I will not move until they recede
back into the forest: huge arboreal swans.

II.
Woodpecker, coffin builder, whenever
I've asked you for a timeline, you've turned away,

showing only your ashen shoulders and blood-
stained head, favoring again the reticence

of hemlocks. I'm certain it was you who wrote
the secret liturgical calendar, entitled *The Nails
of Days*. Bony shafts of sunlight pin me to the forest
floor, a half-conscious object, inevitably

consigned to sleep. Woodpecker, coffin builder
fly from your lifeless cedar, join me

in the green decay. Come see these half-free
morels that have sprouted a tiny graveyard

on this path to the abandoned dollhouse
where I was born.

ODYSSEUS IN VERMONT

Having crossed Lake Champlain with his giddy fleet, he sensed
the real perils would appear on land. Green hum of the earth,
pine spruce cedar moss sedating the horses and sailors, who
longed to rest in every meadow and nap amongst the goldenrod.
Odysseus prodding them into the hills, with tales of sweet syrups,
herbed honeys and amber with the sheen to rouse courtesans
and muses. They drove their chariots through pond-dappled valleys
the clear sky reflected in the blue eye of each lake like hopeful prophecies.
Riding through the stillness's of limestone and granite where
the Abenakis left moon-round faces and deer-heads to beckon favor
from their gods. They paused to watch Bald Eagles skywrite versions
of their dreams, then stopped to re-supply in a village where miner,
miller, plowmen, haberdasher, barber, forester, barkeep, farrier
all welcomed them and sent them on their way with wheels
of cheddar, seeded breads, casks of red and tawny ales. What
troubled Odysseus were the literal signs in plywood nailed askew
to tree bark: **SWEATERS FOR SALE TURN RIGHT**—with a flying arrow.
SCARVES & SHAWLS—THIS WAY. Gifts, he knew his men
would wish to carry home to their wives and lovers. Though what
most unsettled him were the lucid tones flowing from their cottages,
a cavernous music sifting through the treetops, reminding him of Circe
and the melodies of the warp weighted looms. So serene the singing,
the ospreys knelt lamenting in their nests and a parliament of owls
roosting in an oak, swung upside-down from its branches. With eyes
closed, Odysseus awoke to old visions of Calypso and her other fine
weavers who wove scarlet and lapis lazuli into the colors of the world,
his body turned into her golden shuttle. While within every stand
of maples he'd entered, he sensed the fresh sap rising all around him.

NEAR ACTAEON'S QUARRY

Mourning finds its measure in the distance one is kept
from splendor. *Stay away, away-away* cautions the arriving eddies

that curl silkily around her thighs, encircle her proficient hips
and flows in an arch around her silvered torso. She's there

in the pearl-gray dawn, bathing in an unnamed quarry, splashing
happily, content to play alone. Swells of chilled water filling her

pitcher that she pours over herself, anointing. It's hunting season:
the time of year when dogs and men are most akin—ravenous

with their ceaseless craving. I too wish I could bear her a child,
rinse her long smooth back or from afar preserve her in ink, in

rhythmic verse. Still, other gods impart: one has yet to live
whom by beauty has not been torn apart. I hear the deer—gifted dancers

leap through the surrounding woods. I won't pursue them,
fearing they'll lead me to her, and this cobalt pen is my only arrow

PEARL BRIDGE

I slipped from shoreline below the Pearl Bridge into
the frigid river. My manic mind mired by the incorrect
time unchanging on the tower clock above the Masonic
Temple. Pulled from the churning currents I heard
my rescuers chuckle when one of them whispered,
"natural cryogenics" for the cold had cast an ice veneer
around my frigid body. Gazing through my glistening
lashes I saw the incandescence of all that is mortal; what
Rodin might have seen as he sought to carve the ideal
embrace: how marble like bone retains a porous silence,
that flourishes within us, that we cannot fathom.

TAPESTRY

Beyond the natural fencing of dense pines,
within the *hortus conclusus*

of birches, I glimpsed a newborn unicorn
in a crib of silken grass.

Its lone horn emerged torqued
as a cerith.

I watched him strain to stand on earthly legs,
unsteady as infants are

with first words. The humid night holding
the sodden moon aloft

to help the wise, nearly blind pearlescent moths
to find their way,

to bringing notice of the wondrous
to every bone-white door.

FREE ZUCCHINI

Nothing like a summer drive with the sunroof open.
The FM disc jockeys all suddenly turned psychic
because they know you want to hear Tom Petty and
the Heartbreakers, The Eagles with Jackson Browne,
Neil Young backed by Crazy Horse, John Prine, Van
Morrison, and every blissed-out artist who ever recorded
"Wooden Ships." On August days off with no rush to be
anywhere, I let the Routes call to me: 8, 47, 63.
My mind is a jubilant bingo machine. Everything now
heartening: kids obliviously riding 10-speeds, teen
skate-boarders who pretend they're surfing in Hawaii,
the simulacrums of the soft-swirl cones like earth-bound
minarets. Yellow, green, red and orange peppers offered
at a roadside stands like still-life cornucopias. Even the
slowest of drivers—seniors like my father going 20 in a 40
cannot fracture my imperturbable peace. Or the parent
doing 5 to 10 below the speed limit, transporting toddlers.
All good I think, all good, especially when I'm stuck
behind a bumper-stickered beater whose politics I totally
concur with: FREE LEONARD PELTIER, FREE
MUMIA, FREE TIBET. Drivers with a liberal, globalized
consciousness—the way I like to view myself. That is,
until I pass those homes with a cardboard box left close
to the curb and a sign that reads: FREE ZUCCHINI.
I think what total bullshit! To disguise what one wants
to be rid of as benign generosity. What a joke, when
every neighbor knows too well the horrors of unregulated
growth. Those grotesque mutations springing from every
rural garden: misshapen truncheons, odd dildos, miniature
bats created for a sport without players. Such a downer
on an otherwise perfect day: a long swim across Puffer's
Pond, bulbs on sale at the local nursery—Dutch Iris and
Parrot Tulip. Do me a favor and pack up that vegetable
everyone within a thousand miles already has more than
enough of. Say a prayer for each green monster (not
the wall at Fenway), and put an the end to this stupidity.
Now turn your back like a happy bride holding her bouquet

148

at the wedding party and toss each humongous zucchini
one by one by one over your white lace shoulder, and onto,
Lord help us, your stinking, wholly organic compost.

COMMANDMENT COUPLETS

God
admonished

the suburban home-
owners:

*Woe to those
who do not mow.*

THE FEEDING

In our high-rise galley kitchen we labor side-by-side covertly taking measure.
You'll always be petite, although it's not dissuaded you from

brandishing utensils. In soup-season such pleasure, watching as you run
the blender: half savage, half manic—chopping slabs of squash,

pureeing lentils. After cooking soup we sit before our Japanese ceramic bowls;
hunch and slurp, our heads bowed towards the rising vapors.

Two anchorites without a want for words nor any sound except the snow
whirling past our night-filled window, down among the brownstones.

III. SHORELINES

Coastal Daisies, Jonesport Maine

The dirt road to the harbor is bordered
by copious daisies. Floral discs absorbing
sunlight, swaying like cheerful drunkards.

They gesture when I pass in that slowness
when I'm stunned by all things that brighten
the world. How these petals mimicking pliant
wings bonded to a dot of sun. Walking inland

I hear the daisies laughing at this foolish man,
then return to contemplation: transmitting
their radiance back towards the sun.

NORTON ISLAND HAIKUS

Wet seaweeds go *pop*
pop pop pop under my boots—
nature's bubble-wrap.

Purple iris bows
from its stage in the meadow.
Tall grasses applaud.

What is it that you
light within me, buttercups
glinting in the sun?

Buddha-pinecone in
dark forest meditation,
wakened by raindrops.

Seagull shadows swift.
Human shadows: ponderous.
Remembering time...

The bell that woke me:
bell of my death. You, dawn bell
sail on without me.

Our boat soon to leave
the dock. The light-struck daisies
do not wave goodbye.

The outgoing tide
unveils blue-white shell-beds, this
grieving underneath.

THE WATCHER

watches hardbound books slide down
the sloped coastal rocks into the drifting

nets of foam, the inlet winds opening each
book near its midpoint, lifting one single

page upright into a sail. Each boat without
a single occupant though atop each deck:

one wooden oar the length of a finger,
an anchor the size of a matron's brooch,

a coil of rope whose entire existence is
replicating a zero. Each thing distinct as I

peered through this oddest pair of binoculars
carved from a block of clear quartz crystal.

SEAHORSE

Hung-over, in bed
I keep my eyes closed.
And they drift by like great silences...

What do you think you are doing down there?
You can hardly swim, hardly
Flee.

Thank God, your bones
Are on the outside of your body, and nobody
In your world loves the taste of a mouthful of bones.

When I die
Don't send the angels for me.
Spare the lies, the roses, the patent leather shoes.

Send me a seahorse I can sail away on...
I'd gladly trade this loneliness
for another

ISLAND PINE SONG

Each morning along the coastal path I'd pick up a random mussel-shell and carry it with me the entire day. Despite irregularities and variations, each shell fit the center of my palm like a well-framed painting. Their blue-white colorations reliably calming like those talismans known to ward off evil eyes. Each day each shell felt more and more like the hand of a small child as I walked the pine-forested trails through pointillism's of sunlight. The first time I heard the boy's voice he happily shouted, *let's pretend!,* which meant it was time for me to ask him what else a mussel shell could be? *A beautiful spoon for feeding babies,* he said. *A toy boat made of pearl that cannot float except when touched by moonlight.* My last night on the island I asked the boy how he'd survived as an orphan. For awhile we sat without speaking, atop a hump-backed rock. Our legs dangling close to the incoming tide. *There are many types of blindness* he replied, *living in a world that one cannot see beyond.* He took two shells from the mound we'd compiled and proceeded to fix an indigo sphere over each of his closed eyelids. Then he took my hand and led me back to the interior.

THE MILK SHORE

Along a stretch of boulder-strewn coast, it was odd
to see just one type of debris. Too numerous to count
but their common identity was apparent as their shapes
in quart, gallon and half-gallon sizes. On shoreline walks
I mostly stumble over squashed cans, pint-glass bottles,
broken flip-flops, sneakers, segments of rope, the tiniest
of children's toys. While on this quarter-mile, only plastic
milk jugs colored a ghostly grayish—white like corneal
opacifications—the milky veneer of near blindness.
I don't recall how long I sat in contemplation watching
the tide retreat and the seaweeds emerge from their dim
salons in dreadlocks and cornrows. I was curious to learn
where the fresh milk had traveled from but the labels with
the names of dairies had peeled off like postage stamps
from vintage envelopes. Why this much milk is consumed
on the water is not the actual mystery. Jugs make cheap
buoys. But remind me, how long is the life of plastic?
Marine biologists estimate over 400 years. Or ask a leather-
back or loggerhead turtle who wears a six-pack-carrier
around its neck as a permanent shackle. Ask an albatross
that mistook a plastic bag for a blossoming squid. For it's
too late to query the grey whale whose diet included duct
tape, golf balls, and surgical gloves apropos for an autopsy.

THE ECHOES OF THE SWANS

In the middle of the lake
nine Whooper swans and no other gods.

A man walks to the shore at dusk
where the rushes tilt and sway

then turn into a shoji screen
behind which, a long-departed love

gradually undressed
one last time before she vanished.

The swans retreat further out
as soon as he arrives.

The man stands there enthralled
listening as they call

to the last cresting silver wave
as it devoured by the blackening night.

Leaving the shore, he moves
his flashlight beam from sand and stones

onto the asphalt road, listening
still to the echoes of the swans as they

soften the air like the sound her
white-silk garments dropping to the floor.

FROM A SHORELINE PORCH IN OREGON, 5:45AM

All that was visible was one light on the lake.

A lantern knotted to a sinewy pole or gripped
in the fist of a boy who held it in between his

wide eyes and the waves. I supposed it was a father
and son who'd come to haul the night fish in.

Or that they'd simply wished to be far away,
to float drifting nowhere in the heightened quiet.

It was an hour before sunrise as I stood barefoot
on the back porch, sensing I was nearing

an end—the end of a jetty or a pier—
a horizontal straightness jutting miles and miles

over small stones and ashen sands.
As the first trace of a daylight appeared

on the bottom of the horizon—a gleaming line
above the eastern shore. I felt the new

morning begin to seep into the lakeside
valley, my pores opening like minuscule flowers

porous to the dew-moist air. I didn't move
a muscle or a bone as I stood watching

the flat-glass surface of the glowing lake.
I, in the stillness, absorbent

as a Rothko canvass stained to its margins
and beyond them in lavender and purple.

IV. THE SCALDING AND THE SCARING

Maples in November

To appear and vanish are
equivalent mysteries.

White-shingle New England house
sunk in a moat of red leaves.

In a fallen world, the fallen leaves
are reminders of severed hands

How time and men engage
in equivalent horrors.

CLEAR-CUT LAMENT

A mountain route through clear-cut slopes
I think only one word: *denuded.*

Stark—the absences of trees, hectares lay fallow,
an emptiness that chainsaws left.

On far-off switchbacks, I hear the logging trucks
shift gears. Terrifying echoes

of grinding rumble. According to new figures
on *housing starts*, "The Economy," like

a body deathly ill, "should gradually recover,"
especially with the climbing demand

for hardwoods coming from Beijing. Forest
life follows ghostly in each diesel

fuel wake. Gray Wolves, Red Foxes, Long-
Eared Owls. Towards Denver, inside this rented

thin-skinned Kia, one disconsolate,
meditative mind, rattled by homeless winds.

COMPLINE IN LATE APRIL

It's still too cold for the crickets
to start chattering

though the seated man leaning
towards the orange flames of his woodstove,
hums softly to himself, as if the sounds
emerging from inside him had arrived
from a distant elsewhere.

The porcelain moon is a shining plate
above his snow-packed roof.
One Boreal owl roosting in
a front yard oak, sounds
twelve notes

which summon him back to
this secret life.

NOT THE BOWL THAT WE FILL BUT THE BOWL THAT WE SERVE

Each morning as we arrive for breakfast, a wooden bowl
awaits us. *Polished Birdseye Maple* with its whirling grain
that mirrors the rivers' swiftness and the head-motions
of horses bolting across the sky. Bowl filled to capacity,
about to spill over with *Melba, Paula Red, Yellow Transparent*—
offerings from a northern summer, crowned with scented
pears: *Anjou* and *Golden Comice*. I want to thank the orchard-
keepers whom we will never know and the bowl itself turned

on a lathe in the same rotation as the stars, and the painter
who will ask to borrow this bowl and place it at the far edge
of a still-life—one form within a small muted canvas; once
finished will begin its just sentence of outliving its creator.
Each apple with its topographic flawlessness, its solemnity
equal to a window through which the August sunlight passes.
Enter the bleached silence of the studio: pear, apple, walls
dipped in sunny blankness. The artist returning to work

touches the dried palette, the arid acrylics clotted like scabs
atop the wound the unhealed world is. Pear and pear-shadow
in respite on a pinewood table. The painter uncertain if one
should attempt to condense clarity, not only the skin-glow
of each form, but their splotches and bruises. Deceptive are
the guises of timelessness, for stillness is never motionless.
Always, an incessant stirring where abundance and annihilation
merge in core and surface, in the sugars of each decay.

BODY SONGS

We are like the sheep that love to lay their bodies in thick grass
as the scent of hay and apples rises coolly off the lake.

We often walk the firm mud shore and watch as wind gusts
stretch their rippled sheets across the surface

for earth is our impenetrable bed. In the morning before light,
in the evening before dark, your heart becomes

a thawing torch. We'll be back tomorrow once the sheep
have huddled close, prepared for wailing winds

and pelting rains. When they bleat, I'm reminded of your voice
in pre-dawn dreams and during love. With coffee

poured in cobalt mugs, we'll stand on the porch and gaze up
at the morning moon till it disappears. We who wish

to sense a kinship with sheep that love to rest their bodies
in rain-soaked meadows, in grasses plush and deep.

DISCS OF A HUNDRED SUNS

Walking after sunrise from concrete sidewalk to flagstone path and onto
a powdery-soft dirt trail, we found nothing brighter than the petals of daises
like dove-wings clinging to the discs of a hundred suns. The artist *among us,*
 speaking of Albers' "Homage to the Square: With Rays," said *all forms are
dying forms* after having left leaving a birch grove in its solemnly exuberant
ballet Whiter only than clusters of wild daisies was a somnambulist Madonna
land-locked in a churchyard lawn. How her alcove traced in outline forms
a keyhole for the child who aches to disappear from the quotidian. Before
descending back to town, the artist knelt then touched the ground where
sunlight touched it and said unbidden, *the way through the body leads nowhere.*
No one asked him what he meant, but passing the church on our way home
I thought how I wanted to grasp what Mary is saying when she is silent,
why loss adheres to flesh and marrow and her downcast gaze pervades
the summer grasses as if the earth itself will never matter.

V. THE LENGTHENING DAYS

Thaw

The winter horse
bends to pull a few
blades of grass
                    poking up
through the cover of
thin snow.
                    I have
not seen you
for so long a time.

READING LIGHTS

I admire the summer moths—
their steadfastness, their obsessions with intense light,
their gray-white wings like desiccated paper, tiny leaflets aflutter

on the midnight porch. And how once
they've opened, their patterns become picture books
adored by small children, books that enchant without any words.

You always fall asleep before me
and I do not want to wake you. Instead, I keep
our bedroom curtains slightly parted, welcoming inside

a wedge of portico light, just enough
radiance to read by. Me, the poor sleeper who
often ends up reading through more than half the night.

I turn each page carefully, soundlessly
so not to disturb you. And sometimes squint
before the fading lines like the old man I'll soon become.

READING JIMENEZ IN MERC FARM MEADOWS, WEST DORSET, VERMONT

The lumber wagons are already there—unhitched, weathered
to a faintly luminous gray by sun and wind,
nearly soft as woven cotton.

No one has carted logs down these slopes for over fifty years.
Homesteaders abandoned their cabins to the silence of mosses
spread across slates and timbers.

Beige horses grazing unperturbed through the warm afternoon,
nonchalantly groom one another as if they still remember
a time they were ridden by warriors and gods.

I loaf for hours reading in a disused cart where birch logs once
laid heavily as scrolls that refused unfurl their secrets.
The books' woven pages familiar to the touch:

Pueblo Nuevo, one-century old, collapsing topography and time.
Smoke echo starlight. Distant voices lighthearted children
skipping down the mountainside.

BIRDHOUSE FOR THE JOYFUL LIFE

The Dorset, Vermont birdhouses with elongated steeples
set atop tall pedestals are little dwellings built for prayer.
Each one centered upon a mown green-summer lawn.
I want one even smaller that will seamlessly fit inside my chest
or another even littler that will snugly hold the two domes
& two ponds of my heart as bevies of vivid birds ceaselessly
arrive and depart. Squalls of yellow in goldfinch and warbler,
the lightness of the white-winged doves, alighting as they did
upon the sack-clothed limbs of St. Francis as he stood
with arms spread wide to emulate the crucifixion
while calling towards his penitent heart the onrush of song.

CICADAS MATING

After their seventeen-year silence
they return to deafen us,
to incite another type of listening:

having remained alive
through the long seasons
of the unsaid.

The word much like the egg,
craving its own birth.
Egg

of a single word,
re-entering the earth,
then waiting.

YOUNG BUCKS AT DAYBREAK

Through the early morning mist
you might glimpse them

as they emerge
from the thickets,

crossing quietly
into the wildflower meadow,

young buck by
young buck.

Each one standing
in the open

bowed, feeding
on dew-bent grasses.

Their bodies
translucent in the dawn

except for
their antlers—

branches they
might leave for you

      to shape into
      a crown of thorns.

THE LILAC HOURS

Lying beneath the bountiful sprays
I heard voices filtered through the sunlight,

heard late spring grasses
building generous fences, that withheld

nothing and keep nothing out:
chiaroscuros of wren and sparrow passing over.

Adrift within the lilac hours, each stem bloomed
into the shape of a frilly microphone.

A crowd of recorders gathered, waiting
for a statement that might never come.

LAST SHOVEL

lies rusting beside the garden
in the gentlest of summer rains.

He sits on his porch
in his Adirondack chair

and listens for the whispers
of melons, broccoli, kohlrabi—

the steady imperceptible ripening
of their lives and his own.

Already, green shoots
have started to sprout around

its wooden body, gathering
like pilgrims for old prayers.

DJ'S & REDEEMERS

It was eerie that Sunday morning, driving north into remotest Maine.
Most of the two-lane State roads seemed deserted. Looking one half-

mile back in my rearview mirror—not a glint of a sun struck fender
nor shimmer of liquefied fire spread across a far-off windshield. Ahead,

little more than Lots For Sale, flea markets without sellers or buyers,
a peculiar museum that charged no admission to view an exhibition

of rusted barnyard implements. I was almost expecting to pass a burnt-out
tank or crashed B-52 circa Vietnam—signs a hideous war had ended.

Only the voices of faraway DJ's eased my apprehension that the world
was not intact, near or elsewhere. On the stations I managed to tune-in,

I listened to a steady diet of classic rock. Except one station in the 107's
with a predilection for metal: Black Sabbath, Anthrax and AC/DC

and one college channel in the 88's sounding quite urbane, exhuming B-
side tracks from The Strokes and the Stones titanic catalog. Later on,

slicing through thick static, I found a Sunday-morning-only-show featuring
the truest blues from Howl 'in Wolf and Son House to Pinetop Perkins—

the ideal companion through the densely deciduous landscape. Then
somewhere in between Belfast and Macias, I imbibed a raucous playlist

of what some folks out this way probably considered *sin*: Blue Oyster
Cult, Dire Straits, Van Halen, Husker Du. For moments I found myself

in a groove, nodding like some possessed bobble-head doll, doing my best
Beavis & Butthead imitations, and nearly overcome with bliss when at

first glance it seemed the Ellington Wal-Mart was permanently deserted.
Driving on, I began to notice parking lots set on random hillsides, filled

to capacity and fronted with pristine signs that led to *The River of God,*
The Solid Rock Worship Center, The High Praise Lighthouse, The Joyful Harvest.

And surmised that some of the parishioners inside who knelt or leapt, enrapt
within, would gleefully declare the ruination of my soul. True, I've never actually

grasped what discriminates the Apocalypse from Armageddon nor the respective
Hells' that allegedly follow. But I figured the State troopers and the local police

were either down on their own penitent knees (posed like those they've arrested)
or were standing with their arms widespread absorbed in praising, crying out

Hallelujah! or maybe even speaking discernibly in tongues. Freeing me to press
my Jesus-leather-sandal-to-the-pedal and gun-it straight for Nova Scotia—

RED LIST LAMENTATION

Bacteria, oxygen, cellular life, the sponge—our briny mother, giant scorpions
who revealed the functions of the fingers, sharks and other fish with jaws,
the first trees and wingless insects including the spider, deer golden as those
who traveled beside Artemis to childbirths and the one who Sita yearned for
in exile, edible pigs born in sties and in the arms of magnificent singers. Cats,
clams, rhinoceros, and once the swamps appeared: crocodile, frog and turtle.
Milk-giving bats that underwrote our primitive brains hanging inverted
in darkness. Sheep, bear, mouse, cow, rat amidst the first seed-sprouting flowers
leading indirectly to our mortal seed and a green path that unlocked paradise.
Columbine, morning glory, pear and grape, orchids like those Darwin nourished
in his hothouse, colossal lilies.
                    Before this current <u>Red List</u> of what is vanishing:
the passenger pigeon that was simply too tasty came to its demise in 1914
in a zoo in Cincinnati, the South African quagga—a caramel-brown zebra,
apparently delicious and with a durable hide for coats and shoes was last seen
in an Amsterdam zoo in 1883, the last Great Auk on the Scottish coast
was executed for witchcraft, the headcount of the Costa Rican golden toad
in 1988 totaled zero, the Baiji White Dolphin frolicked in the Yangtze
until 2008 and left the young eco-poets adrift in moonlit rowboats, weeping.
Theories reason that blades, darts and harpoons took the woolly mammoth
and sabre-tooth cat. And in ensuing eras, creatures were slaughtered by scythe
and hoe—implements also used in recent genocides, along with the machete.
In century-twenty-one, both Blue Whales and Giant Pandas nearly disappeared.
Crop monoculture, habitat degradation, human induced climate-change
and -borne invasive species reside beneath the grim umbrella of *biocide:*
a weaponless assault of ultraviolet radiation from a thinning ozone layer,
increased use of pesticides, habitat loss from agri-business and citification,
invasions of alien species, the exotic wild-life trades in aphrodisiacs
and tusks, light pollution, fungal disease.
                    The patrolled borderlands between Mexico
and the USA are threats to bison, jaguars, Sonoran pronghorn and Mexican
wolves who migrate by dark without passports among illicit families and workers
trying to cross or re-cross with nothing but plastic water jugs. Ecosystems of
fence and wire spell trouble for the mountain bear and tiger—neither pious
nor xenophobic that live on the India/Pakistan border. Our geologic record
construes *the present* time as sixty-six million years. Time unchanged, passing
inside us from sleep to sleep, love to love.

FOR I DREAMT OF THE GODS OF ICE AND FIRE

The reflections of the trees in the ponds
will be all that is left of the trees.

And the streams—bereft of fish will be
the final place where humans go
to deposit the gold eggs of memory.

The winds will rush crying
across the scared lands

in search of another home—
signaling the end of music.

This epoch to be known
as The Triumph of the Dust

where each alone will scavenge earth
among other nameless shadows.
Each shadow doomed to wander

lost and downcast, famished
for the bitter, bitter earth.

POEM IN HONOR OF THE 50TH ANNIVERSARY OF THE NAVAJO CODE-TALKERS

Sending messages the Japanese could not decode.
Whale equals battleship. Potato stood
for hand grenade. Egg meant bomb.
A language dreamt up by the Pentagon.
Years later, On Black Mesa no need
for codes. Strip mine means strip mine,
leases for mineral rights, fence between Navajo
and Hopi where no fence was before,
termination of sheep, relocation of elders
to cinder block malls. Hiroshima was
rebuilt, but if you go to Black Mesa
the mine pits are larger than the holes
from bombardments. Peabody Coal is not
the code name for sacred ground. Ask the sons
of Navajo veterans dying young,
much younger than the half-life of uranium.

SMALL SONG FOR STANDING ROCK

Under the Missouri River under the Missouri
light crude, light sweet crude.

Viscous tar-pitch-black through pipelines
to be laid beneath the tribal river, the pure river.

There are surface treasures etched into our planet:
sunlight on the surface of the flowing river,

bird life on-around-above the flowing river—
gull, eagle, pelican, tern. Their maps do not show

where rubber bullets bruised the human skin,
where German Shepherd's growled then bit,

where tear-gassed eyes wept toxic tears. 570,000
barrels will surge each day beneath Lakota lands.

No one can predict a future break, an unseen
seepage, a sudden leak before fouled waters reach

one child's lips and all the lips and mouths and throats
that voiced their love and sorrow for the river,

their anguish for the land, for the buffalo snuffed out
one century ago. There's almost no one left

at Standing Rock encampment to protest, to ensure
old treaties will be honored. Only for now, only

for today, may we safely drink from the Missouri.
Drink with tranquil hearts and minds

until Sunoco comes for the light sweet crude—
one-half million barrels every day.

THE FAILURES OF THE ARK

"And the waters prevailed exceedingly upon the earth; and all the
high hills that were under the whole heaven, were covered." —Genesis 7:19

No rain for most of summer. Withered gardens. Seared grasses. Infestations
of grasshoppers and crickets like those known from scriptural plagues. Only
a one jet ski crossing Lake Memphremagog with the price of gasoline

an inflated pleasure. Driving inland on back roads through New England,
one passes boats moored in weedy lots, perched on cinderblocks, in driveways
set on rusted hitches as if shipwrecked in mid-air. A peculiar sight unless these

landlocked vessels will soon be operative as arks teeming with weaving spiders,
with woodpeckers enlivened by their own percussion, with hundreds of mourning
doves as they build new nests from sticks and twigs, assembling our final heaven.

TO A SMALL COPPER BUTTERFLY

I've only ever known you as a replica
of the heart, tiny lyre, book of smoke.
I listened to you breathing once you
settled on my wrist as if the mortal
pulse is nectar, then watched as you
passed above my lolling body—a silk
fan painted with a bamboo footbridge
leading into distant, mist-shrouded
mountains. By the malachite river
you fluttered over me like a skilled
hand suturing a wound. Your antennae
soundless as the nothingness of
your song. I will leave this shining
riverbank with you, going wherever
you go. I sense we aren't far, *Lycaena
phlaeas*, whom the Greeks referred to
as a *burning flower*. The heft of these
massive fallen trees anesthetized by
sunlight. I understand now, why you
brought me to this hidden infirmary
of maple, linden, oak and pine—all
slumped, collapsed, keeled over.
And among them, one plain casket:
open, unoccupied, filled with light.

ANTIQUE JEWELRY

The black beetle trundling in sunlight
through the mica-flaked roadside dirt
was an actual locket.

Peeling back its carapace
revealed a porcelain cameo
of my mother's posthumous face.

VI. COLD AGAIN

The Blakean Sky

For days on end I stood beneath dense clouds.
Detached beards of martyrs and prophets—
hoary whirlpools portending wrathful silence.

Saints, hermits, ghost-penitents
notorious for their cavernous hoods, staffs, rods and crooks
suturing the air above the dung-scented fields.

I watched clouds gather, forming an inverted well—
a portal of sapphire that summoned me
to launch myself through its eye unblinking.

WHAT THE OWL ADVISED NEAR THE END OF AUTUMN

No time
to feel bereft.

Each one of us

is midwife
to our death.

No time

to be
bereft

with each of us

a midwife
to our

death.

LAST BRIDGE

At first I noticed small clouds
windblown into letters, then syllables,

then an encoded message he accepted
as its recipient. A jumble of *g's, r's, a's*

and *e's,* and one *t* like a little crucifix
he wanted to read as *grace* and *gratitude.*

No sooner had he finished deciphering
the cottony scrawls they'd realigned

into a Taoist hexagram he didn't know
how to interpret until he recognized

that suite of chest x-rays his oncologist
pinned before him in an orderly row

delicately backlit as the photographed
phases of the moon. Bones

with shadows whirling inside them
like bamboo poles assembled into a bridge

that links the cloud-covered mountains
where the hermit unseen, will cross alone.

WAKING IN A MOTEL ROOM FROM AN EARLY EVENING NAP

to the steady thrumming of Vermont rain.
Eyelids open

to an unfamiliar ceiling.
The coffin's inner lid is never far away.

IN THE MIND OF THE DYING

dangles
an image:

a frayed rope
of frailly

connected words
grasped

weakly
as the mind

rappels down
the glass cliff

of consciousness
till another

voice (not
his own)

murmurs—
let

go.

LEGACY

Tonight I will orate
to the moon—

to its empty pews
and casket-shadows.

Reciting at a murmur
my final will-

and-testament,
where those in attendance

inherit
fallen starlight.

ROADS BUILT AT SUNRISE

I woke in prismatic light like a crystal newly pulled from earth
        then saw a glass house weightless in the center of a slate-blue lake.

        I thought it almost possible to walk upon the surface, to follow
        one of its transparent roads once sunup drew its lanes upon it.

ANOTHER WEALTH

The swallows of Anamekerig
swerve through the silvery twilight

as if following invisible racetracks
in the sky. The flawless

spheres they travel pre-drawn
by ecstatic compasses.

Spirits swift in flight—freer
than the fleetest thoroughbreds,

whose dapper owners
with their oversized binoculars

pressed against their eyes,
care only to pursue trophy-

gold and the cumbrous
wreaths of blood roses.

LINES TO A VANISHED MUSE

You left a crown of wisteria
in the meadow of spear-tipped grasses.

*

Night after night I called to you
through the tiers of pine branches
that formed trellises overhad
for snowdrops, tears, and stars.

*

The grotto in the heart is the grotto
for the song.

DARK SQUARE

I

DREAMING AND WAKING

We are threatened with suffering from three directions: from our own body, which is doomed to decay and dissolution and which cannot even do without pain and anxiety as warning signals; from the external world, which may rage against us with overwhelming and merciless forces of destruction; and finally from our relations to other men. The suffering which comes from this last source is perhaps more painful than any other.

No one who, like me, conjures up the most evil of those half-tamed demons that inhabit the human beast, and seeks to wrestle with them, can expect to come through the struggle unscathed.
—Sigmund Freud

DOCTOR, PLEASE

A militia of crows has gathered in the yard. I know now what the symptoms
    are. One patient took

a hacksaw to his throat then pulled on the rim of his turtleneck to expose a
    virgin scar. Another man recalled his life

as Perseus, forever cradling a severed head. Snake tongues on the black sun.
    The eyelids flutter.

What happened to the party guests who once dressed up as astronauts? Most
    work on Wall Street; one's

already dead. This early morning waking, the anvil of daybreak waits above my
    head. And what about the young

man who claims he's really Icarus and continues to insist he doesn't belong on
    this planet anymore

because he lost his wings near the surface of the sun. Doctor, please interpret
    what the dream voice said:

Go now and follow the owl stone of dawn. Walk to your waist through the oil.
    Moor the blue rowboat

that drifted off from shore. Their feathers, you can touch them without harm
    although they're drenched in chemicals

and heavy from the tar. Your waterfowl are bound to Earth.
    You must find for yourself another way to soar.

THE INSOMNIAC'S PET SHOP

I have no use for cages.
The gerbils can copulate wherever
they want.

By moonlight, I clean the dead
canary of the birdseed it is lying in,
pluck the pretty feathers—cerulean
and yellow-gray.

With Chopin on the antique gramophone
I savor the skips and scratches,
waltz with the white toy poodle
that sleeps in a wire cell by the window.

In my pet-shop all the fish tanks
are densely laced with algae
no human gaze can permeate.

Buy a goldfish from me—
it's an act of faith.

And maybe, like your own
prayer for rest, you'll hear
the tiny diver
calling you from the bottom.

GRAVITY

She walks into my office, crying.

　　　　　　　　　　　Not her own pet or that of a relative or a
friend but a dog
she'd never seen until yesterday. Her forehead slumps into her hand
as she recalls how this animal hurled itself over the railing
from the Observation Tower that crowns Mount Tom like a party-hat.

The yowling, the pain-filled yelps—I'd never heard anything like it.
She describes the mound of broken, dislocated bones, the four splayed legs
and bleeding snout; the laxness of the rescue workers
and the nonchalant comments of other hikers.
"Should have been on a leash." "At least it wasn't a human life...."

　　　　　　　　　　Returning home to find her mother half-
way through
her second six-pack, gazing soporifically at the autumn dusk
 that loomed behind
Oprah on the TV screen. So she walked across the road to visit a male
neighbor,
who after sympathetically nodding his head,
thought the best form of comfort was to arouse her breasts.

　　　　　　　　　　How should a therapist respond to her clear-
sighted perspective,
that if-nothing-lasts-then-nothing-matters, except to say,
f nothing matters—nothing lasts.
Each of us remote in this late autumnal gloom
with the image of a dog sprawled in flight.

My patient remained inconsolable through the hour
while I silently imagined animated dogs falling
from even greater heights
and alighting back on Earth intact.

Scooby-Doo, Underdog, Pluto. Childhood Sunday mornings
lounging on the carpet beside my sister. Waking in the Sunday dawn
to watch Davey and Goliath. Always one or the other
burdened with regret
for their animal deficiencies and mortal failures.

Next we'd watch The Jetsons, an intergalactic
family
with a dog named Astro, inhabiting a universe
where I often wished to live:
buoyant in a world without gravity.

THE BOUNDARIES

"...and I must save them, High fires will help"
—John Berryman, *Dream Song 131*

Rebecca the angelic Greek had tributary scars coursing up and down her arms. Sharon with the waist length hair redder than a fire truck and skin Kabuki-pale would light a cigarette, take one drag or two, then extinguish it against her breast. Holly was a sweetheart, her sketchbooks filled with self-portraits in the nude: Pastels with thighs spread wishbone-wide to point where the damage had transpired. "Terror, does it emanate from outside or within?" Fine question Sarah, but why now do I think of Berryman falling toward his end? All these students traumatized by violence and neglect. Liz explained, after years of being groped and probed, she'd watch her hands in dreams turn gangrene—her fingers fall off one by one. How many others have sat squirming in that leather chair, sinking, as they mumbled, "When the ground gave way, I crumbled." But tell me, Mr. Bones, what true words might I utter to the chronically bereft? What about her fantasy, its better after death? Maureen watched her stepfather drag her mother by the hair like a pull toy. "The guy was really crazy when he drank. A trichotillomaniac in reverse. Even worse, when he picked me up from school, instead of driving home, he'd detour to the woods, demanding that I show him how I eat an ice-cream cone, but to do it on his dick." "When I was bleeding," Jennifer made clear, "my mother's boyfriend wouldn't want to fuck. He'd spit into my face and scream, What a dirty little bitch! Then take revenge on my pet rabbits, slit one throat and order me to cook it for his supper." What now might I say to offer comfort? Men are more despicable than ogres. Given only a diploma and the language tool, I started to uncover all these girls alive beneath the rubble. Carrie described how her stepbrother would crawl into her bed at night purring like a kitty cat. "He'd lick me head-to-toe, cleaner than a milk bowl, then leave his glue-white puddle on my breast". A doctor resolute in mind. I wouldn't touch you ever, except in dreams and only with my eyes for I too want to heal and live again. Spirit-loss, possession by ghost, symptoms in a diagnostic book. What Henry aptly labeled, the horror of unlove... Lord knows, how many times I found you crouching in the scum, huddled at the bottom of a well. It's madness, insists the doctor in his notes, to descend without a lantern or a thread- -taking nothing with us but the will. Though Jeanette said it better near the end of one sad session, "Some walls are made of love."

185

CUTTERS

Not wood, not stone,
not apple or bread,
not Thanksgiving
turkey or Easter pig;
the cloth she cuts
is her own flesh.
She arrives
on the unit
and I search her
for safety
pins, sewing
needles, pencils
with points,
mirrors concealed
inside compacts.
In group therapy
one patient said,
"a razor blade
is better than sex,
the blood flow
more soothing
than warm milk
with honey."
Cutters sense
the skin as
testament, ruined
palimpsest,
marking lines
like an Etch
A Sketch
till blood
bubbles up
like a hot spring.
If only she could
ripen, peel herself
from her body
I could help;

before she's led,
wrists
scrolled in
gauze,
into isolation,
beyond the dead
bolt doors.

WOLF TRAP

One forelimb gnawed
through the marrow.

Blood drool in a puddle
on the tongue.

In the hospital dark
calling to the lifelines

on the dove-white ceiling,
wherein the mind

does one go to
release the damaged parts?

Don't cry wolf.
Cry to the bone.

Cry milk.
Or sing

of the un-cracked tundra
that she was.

SNOW

Each flake is an old Cape Cod church
with its steeple splintered off.

Still, it is possible
to locate a hymn within.

I was handed a thin
porcelain implement by a man

prepared to die.
He said they are alike

the baton of the maestro,
the white stick of the sightless.

LEAVING PARK STREET STATION

Heart wrecked in a dismal year. Too many godless
Boston Sundays benched at the harbor's edge, waiting
for another tugboat's woeful moan, one more broken

vessel dragged in for repairs. In subway glass a ghostly
face appeared: crow lines beneath the eyes, lips cracked
like the scales of a haddock. Deserted by words, I couldn't

even ask myself, how many fractures must the mind endure
before it's finely jigsawed? Nearing dusk, I'd meander
home through the narrow sidewalk chatter of Portuguese

and Haitians: neighbors, teenage lovers, Big Wheels, ghetto
blasters. Though sometimes in the twilight I'd
let myself go beyond the stop at Central Square and ride

the T all the way to Alewife. Arriving at the end, almost
calmed by the steady fluorescent hum. The last passenger sitting
in a vacant car, relieved at not having to go any farther.

THE EMBRACE

The orderlies know he is asking
for this:

to be pinned down
as he bites, head-bangs,

spews expletives,
enraged as they wrestle him

into a skintight suit
like those worn

by divers
about to plunge

backwards
into the frozen sea.

Later, in the staff room
jotting chart notes,

I admire the empty straitjacket
flaccid on the gurney.

Strap me down
under buckle & belt.

Hold me.

COURAGE

All morning the white vans arrive with potted plants
and flowers. I feign having a relative here and tell
the receptionist I'm looking for my younger brother.

"That kid decked out in leather who flew like a giant bat
Above the windscreen of his Harley and now can't make
a fist or talk." Corridors of invalids re-learning how to

walk and swallow as OT's and PT's urge them on: Just one
more step. Lift your spoon. How many heroes in this
one building? How many minds repeating, Why go on?

> Youville Rehabilitation Center
> Cambridge, Massachusetts.

DARK REMEDIES

Since our occupation is primarily with the failed aspects of life, we would have to put away all ideas of therapeutic success. If I seem to be making the soul sick again by such stress on pathologizing, I am at the same time giving sickness soul again.
—James Hillman

The day room is a Buddhist shrine.
The morning pills are deities.

Six patients sit with a talk show on
though most are staring into space.

One man stands up suddenly
and hollers—

"Shut up
or else I'll lock you in the closet!"

Another man insists
he's been abducted twice

by Martians, gives a wary,
sidelong glance,

sits tacit
as a fist.

*

These co-eds, Smith-and-Barnard-smart,
interrupted mid-semester from thesis work
on Freud, Muhammad and Jean Arp.

One woman complains, "My skin is
turning blue like a Picasso canvas,

circa 1902. My fingertips feel icy-cold.
My hands look bare-fist-boxer bruised."

A pair of anorexics on the day-room sofa

whisper about refusing food. One teenage girl
looks defeated. She paces the carpet-quiet halls
in socks. Her nostrils leashed to a feeding tube.

*

It doesn't require divination or degree
to see this teenage kid is thinking,
"This is all such bullshit."

Another hour of humdrum psychotherapy:
he's male, Caucasian, fifteen,
defiant, a chronic runaway.

Usually it's easy to accept
a session going nowhere.
We have nothing more to say,

though we're both locked up
by the billable clock
for another nineteen minutes.

Maybe, I should willingly agree
and say, Yes, Alex, you're absolutely right.
Time is hell, and worldly life is crap.

*

At intake, the new admission's face
reveals two befuddled eyes
and an odd, celestial gaze,

suggesting the unsaid
is all he wishes he could say:
Doctor, What remains
after the self
has been demolished?

*

I've seen too many faces peer
down the corridor of mind's

black hole and in a total loss
for words, choke

as if a fish bone
had stabbed the throat.

I understood exactly what it meant:
I am what I fear most.

*

Ringlets of Bermuda onion,
alfalfa sprouts spooled in airy tangles,

the empty retinas of chick peas,
the scarlet eyeballs of cherry tomatoes.

In line at the hospital salad bar,
staring down into the canisters.

I could really use a double
Hennessy on ice.

Madness curbs the appetite.

*

Late again for another patient.
Unconscious avoidance?

Could this be my intention?
"For fuck-sake,"
my firesetter growls,
"get me the fuck out of here."

Where else would you like to be?
I asked him and then myself.

His retort, "Anywhere
But this shit house."
Though I for one wish

I was buckled in an Airbus
on a runway headed for Mauritius or Bali.

Twenty-seven session-minutes left.
I still possess an ounce of tact.
With every caustic accusation:
"Uh-hum, uh-hum," I mutter back.

*

Shared psychotic, catatonic,
oxymoronic, hypomanic,

anyone who soars like Mary Poppins.
In the name of peace

I'll grease their eyes, scrub
their minds and won't confess:

getting well's a magic trick:
One day the brain

is in the clear. The next,
mercurial, fickle, sick.

*

Each man and where he dwells,
in a mousehole of his own design,

unwell. Daily group therapy
with seven schizophrenic males

is not remotely comparable
to bachelors meeting up in Vegas.

Laborious this tick-tick-tick.
The wall clock has a terrible case

of Tourette's. "Would anybody
care to speak?
Speak up. Speak out."

*

After my patient
hanged himself,
I couldn't rest for months.
Distress strung
his frayed noose
invisibly around
my neck. From
blood-shot eyes,
I'd watch black
sky become black
day, aircrafts
blink like sparklers
alighting down
the Boston sky
and sidewalk pigeons
grieving. Sky-
scrapers twinkled
like slender bars
of silver 'til
my frenetic mind
went down
in Valium sleep.
I'll be your plumber and your guide
through pipelines of intimacy revived.

Now let's play
a curative game.

I promise I won't make you dance
to the memories of your abuse.

Or have you shape a ball of clay
into your hateful feelings for your father.

The game we'll play
is called, Pass the Miner's Head Lamp.
For fun
we'll search for truth.

Though we'll need another
prop or two,

especially a top hat
to pull out hope.
Once a week I undertake the role of patient.
My doctor has a fish tank at the entrance
to his office. When he greets me in the waiting
room, I wonder if he's sure they're not piranha?

I don't let on how I'm troubled
by the Miro poster hanging behind his balding head:
spiders, sperm, and raindrops,
red and blue amoebas—entities that madmen claim

lodge inside the cranium. I understand
the dictum, therapist, heal thyself.
But why should my shrink really care what my mother
has in common with my history of lovers?
I think he can see it in my eyes—I'd like to quit
and use the cash for a flat-screen Mitsubishi
or a long weekend in Paris. Subtly, he cautions me:

"You must liberate yourself first, or your life will

amount to nothing but role-play and mockery."
I've insisted more than once, though I might never heal
in accord with the parameters specified in DSM-III,
there are spaces (inside and without) where I can, briefly,
be.

*

Don't forget the report due tomorrow:
What animals and sorrows did she conjure

from the inkblots? What unblemished insights
did he attain when anguishing these verbal hours?
What are her strengths and deficits?
Describe her capacity for friendship.

Include the tragic tales she told about the boy
with the damaged violin, and incest on the farm.

                    *

Once a year for those whose home is "long-term care,"
we offer up an eggnog toast, merriment and cheer.

A choir aloft on high-dose Paxil lines the bleachers
while credentialed men and women, dignified

in trench coats, exhale warmer air into rosy palms
and fidget with sleek leather gloves.
Not often healed and unhealed stand this close together
(almost kin) and (look out from the outside in).

Cold mud, slush, the pill-white snow,
angels hanging upside down, a dozen tongue-less bells.
In a session of art therapy, the patients
are all working hard, praying for

at least a day pass or an overnight
at home for Christmas.

I join them at their lively table
and make a Christmas tree with Elmer's glue

and glitter. The lights on the spruce
burn crimson and beryl as if the remedies

might come. This chill is not
preventable—

it leaks,
it seeps into everyone.

II

THE ORIGINS OF BLINDNESS

Illusions commend themselves to us because they save us pain and allow us to enjoy pleasure instead. We must therefore accept it without complaint when they sometimes collide with a bit of reality against which they are dashed to pieces.
—Sigmund Freud

THE ADOPTION: TRAUMA AND RECOVERY
"far too often secrecy prevails, and the story of the traumatic event
surfaces not as a verbal narrative but as a symptom." —Judith Herman, MD

Below the milk-bell,
floating in the heart-light

alone among the shadows
of your ribs

I wound the bell rope
in my newfound fist.

Hang on
or hang myself and spare us both.

        *

A clear light suddenly fell
on me and I discovered I could

                  drift

amidst the mica chips
that galaxied your eyes.

        *

Who's your mom, you'll never know
While in the cradle to and fro.

Your blessing and your early curse
You'll never nuzzle, never nurse.

Now shriek until your face turns red
My sugar beet, she's probably dead.

Bastard of a lover's tryst
Have patience son, turn loss to grist.

Go forth young soul and part the seas
Now cure those with your disease.

*

In the dream I am a child unwinding

your ophthalmologic bandages,
searching

    for your eyes.

I unwind the gauze
round and round and round.

Nothing but the same white facelessness.

*

MY MOTHER'S MISCARRIAGES

I never saw your river of blood or the two floods
that swept them away from you. Had I arrived
in time I would have stood on the bridge, leaned

over the guard rail, called their unspoken names,
guided their tumbling bodies with my eyes
safely into the ocean where all things are at home

without names. I would have let them live or else
carved their marble tombs with my own whetted rib,
raised thimbles of their ashes to those years of lost

motherhood for I could not offer you an earthly,
healing bread. When the orphan-worker brought me
to your door, you took my name from the New

Testament, as if I could re-write their stories
with my life. Your rock, your church, your indestructible
stone, only time will tow away, not blood, not water.

HELP

"The Negro came to the white man for a roof or for five dollars
or a letter to the judge; the white man came to the Negro for love."
—James Baldwin, "Down at the Cross"

How many childhood nights I walked down the dim stairs
to the basement to sit with you and the sound of the rumbling

dryer, to listen to your stories of tyrants and plantations
as you folded with precise care the underpants of my family.

You who knew our human stains: faint arrowheads of feces
and blood. Often during suppertime, an ungovernable sadness

washed over me as you ate by yourself in the kitchen,
after circling around our mahogany table with bowls of string beans

and tin-wrapped baked potatoes. I never understood why you
couldn't join us in the dining room when every morning you

buttered my toast and placed Oreos and Fritos in my lunch box.
After I left for college, it was you who held Mother every afternoon

as she watched her own mother succumb to the hidden grapes
of malignancy, embracing her beside the kitchen sink while Days

of our Lives flickered in the background. Still, Mother insisted
on disguising you in uniforms of baby-pink and powder-blue,

perhaps to subdue the power of your skin, completely ebony,
except for your palms, lighter, the color of milk chocolate.

Shining hands that entered my sickroom at night
with a washcloth that was cool and a spoon dripping honey.

DOLLS

With dull gold kernels of hard winter corn spread across my palm I recall
playing jacks with my sister on the hardwood kitchen floor. The bright
spiked satellite of each jack as coveted as antique beads. Once after losing,

I stole her Raggedy Ann and dragged the bulky doll in her calico dress
by the carrot-red braid into the woods to bury her not knowing what I
was trying to get rid of. Years later, I'd come upon other dolls heaped

in dumpsters, soil-covered in gardens, and one Kewpie beside an interstate
among the black reptilian skins of fallen retreads. Baby dolls all pudgy
and glossy. Teenage dolls with manes of platinum blonde and perfect

breasts without nipples. I've wondered how a child's doll ends up in a gutter
amputated and dirty, how neglect fits its way into everything,
while their eyes remain so still and crystal-blue, like nothing else on Earth.

PLAYER

There is a game he vaguely remembers that he wants to remember:

A game that girls were especially good at, where an origami
flower turns into a paper mouth which tells the heart's truth.

Pick a number, she'd instruct. Now. . .
pick a color.

Somehow, he understood, simply by playing that he was winning.

He'd study their fulsome mouths, their downcast, angelic eyes, the
smallest hardest curves
of their new breasts, their hushed joy in keeping secrets,
then revealing them.

Though he couldn't comprehend a drop of her theology,
he'd think, Thou art in heaven.

MY SISTER'S GIRL FRIEND

She came uninvited. Self-offering
in flannel nightgown with tiny
sky-blue flowers. No brother at home
to celebrate her flourishing.
I was terrified, too unsettled to touch
her skin as she stepped to the side of my bed
holding the hem of her nightgown
and lifting it up below her breasts
to fan me like a campfire.
Her white smoothness with this
newest tuft more delicate than corn silks,
than seeds of milkweed floating off.

She waited, intent on my attention,
but I was impossible to reach;
so overcome with the desire to touch
all my brain cells went dark.
Once she was certain that I'd studied
the sprouts of her sexual hair—the birth
of the animal and the woman simultaneously,
she galloped off from my shadowy bedroom
like a young gazelle,
swelling with pride and giggling wildly.

TO HEAR THE CHORUS SING

A man alone in the middle of his bed.

His penis rising because it loves
to rise, regardless of what the man
does or does not love. Shifting like
a compass that guides him through
the forest where he is lost.
Pointing upward to remind him to love
the rest of his body, his small, un-nourishing
nipples, the apple in his throat that blocks
his song like a stone.

As he touches
himself, he defies himself: remembers
the luminous mallard clamping
the duck with his bill, and the dragonfly—
long turquoise needle of light
crazed and sizzling pushing her
in delirious circles around the sky,
coyotes crying from hill to hill,
a barn owl carrying in its voice
the first memory of water.

He senses what
swirls and surges through the stomach,
what dips into the testes and sings
is not the blood, but light reaching
for the farthest walls of space
though never reaching them.
And when desire quiets, he settles
like the sleek crescent moon into daylight,
curling fetal into himself,
holding his animal body like a mother

RODIN EXHIBIT ON THE ROOFTOP,
METROPOLITAN MUSEUM OF ART

Caryatid fallen with urn, fallen with stone.
In ancient Greece these women were motionless
columns upholding the roof, sheltering the world.

Above Central Park set free in morning light
they trudge one step per century toward
the blockish skyline. Near Midtown, Atlas

steadies the Earth as my father did, hoisting me
above his head before setting me on his shoulders,
not for a view of helium floats or the sunlit treetops,

but knowing his own equine eyes would soon close
and I would become his true periscope.
From the rooftop of the Metropolitan Museum

I was wanting to glimpse Saint John the Divine.
Wide-eyed saints in upright tombs, posed rigidly
in gestures of certainty. No other women here

burdened with the stones and waters of their fates.
While the burghers stood pensively, welded together
before certain death, surrounded by luscious nudes,

backs arched, breasts bronze and firm. Caryatid,
at least you were blessed with a name
like those of birds: small, quick, yellow, fluttering.

EL MUNDO DEL TERROR

The violence I dreamt of inflicting on others I discovered
watching wrestling on UHF in Spanish. I didn't care
when a friend's older brother informed me it was all a fake
and a hoax: nose rips, eye gouges, ear twists, body slams,
the use of foreign objects, his baritone voice exclaiming,
Rompe! rompe! le cabeza! I was jubilant with my Spanish ally.
Genuine torture. Pleasure at another's expense. I enjoyed
scorching ants with my magnifying glass, their legs singed,
crisped, curling up, turning into smoke. And pleased to see
the bees trampoline on the guts of a roadkill squirrel.
After college, I read Timerman, Hikmet, Wiesel. Torture
on every continent, a tower of memoirs describing terror
reaching towards the stratosphere. And what of those who
never told their stories? Fingers sausaged off and forced
down windpipes, tongues hacked from the backs of throats,
the snapshot faces in a manila folders, skulls in mass and
unmarked graves. Now I wrestle with other violence within
and around me. That boy struggling on his knees, trying to
press his adversary to the ground, to make him eat dirt, to
take no shit from nobody. No one ever again daring to call
him wimp, pussy. And twenty years later on the office carpet,
a six year old, play-therapy patient loads and unloads
a yellow toy dump truck. Welts and scar tissue
inside his anus when he was only wanting to be loved.

TO THE PIER

The star of our sadness rises invisibly through this coldest daylight
as we walk on hardened snow to the pier. The word soon

almost identical to the word son, lacking only the o: the hollowness
of exclamation, the mouth that swallows absence.

The o held in cupped palms like a robin's egg, which we fit inside
like a tomb, how father is missing only the r that turns

you into farther, in consonance with over. Language is distraction.
Our silence twines us in a nautical knot. When we speak

of time dissolved by death our blood ropes hold unbroken. This is
how we progress. Here the waves are never frozen.

BUBBLE

Blowing gently into the plastic zero
he was astonished:

how his breath could yield such delicate orbs
finer than Swarovski glass.

It didn't matter that perfection was transient
for its beauty was repeatable,

effortless as lifting the arm of the turntable
and placing it back at the beginning of the song.

He would stand in the suburban driveway or sit in the backyard lawn,
enclosed in a bubble

of clandestine happiness. Wisps of air emitted
from his lungs

sending the mauve and lilac tinted globes cascading into sunlight.
While somewhere in his mind,

in an outlying place, without signage or roads,
he sees himself still

there: green summer
brimming with dandelions and bumblebees,

the round container in one hand,
a blue wand clasped daintily between his fingers.

Bubbles like winged horses rising bounteous around him and he
rising with them.

III

EROS STRICKEN

Love in itself, in the form of longing and deprivation, lowers the self-regard; whereas to be loved, to have love returned, and to possess the beloved object, exalts.

Where they love they do not desire and where they desire they do not love.
  —Sigmund Freud

PERIOD

I go down on you during your bleeding,
though you insist the fumes that river from your body are the odors
of slaughter, the lamb resigned to sacrifice.
Cramps, headaches, nausea. I bring you
Anaprox with blackberry tea.

In bed when you turn away,
my hands reach out for your dampened shoulders. You say
you're beginning to feel yourself restored by the flowing out.

I see how this letting go
releases you, reminding me why I must enter solitary
spaces whether or not my body decrees me there.
Your blood is deep cherry, plum, cabernet.
Salty roses bloom in the garden beneath you.

BLACKBERRY NIGHT

When I crushed the berries
in my fist,
they bled all over you.

Nipple and navel.
The body knowing
what the mind cannot know:

Faint breezes
skimming the gossamer hairs
along your arms.

Globes of pollen
beyond our windows,
floating off.

Leaning over you
in the dark I carry
blackberries.

Each luscious cluster
from my tongue on-
to your tongue,

careful, not to
crush the meteors
of our slow, tangy joy.

Later, breaking them
bead by sweet bead.
The tart juices

dripping in rivulets
over your torso,
a puddle

in your navel.
Our rosary
scattered, in seed.

EL MUNDO DEL ORO

'There is a world underneath this world,'
you said. Your breasts dangled over me
like cones of honey. What more do you want?

"There is radiance to what is given form.
Put my elbow in your mouth, my ankle, my nipple."
On lunch break I walk the Hartford barrio,

examine the polished chains in the window,
hoops and delicate zeros of gold laid on black
velvet. Last night we spoke of formal gardens:

Tivoli, Versailles. And when I asked how you
prayed, you answered, In Spanish, on my knees
and barely breathing in that sorrowful well

within his heart. In the dimly lit park below
your window, junkies, drunkards and homeless
men lie on benches or crawl inside appliance

boxes without a blanket or a coat, while we are
cozy, curled up knee-to-knee, listening as the snow-
flakes pile quietly along the painted chipped sill.

THE HAPPY SLEEPING BED

When my arm reaches out across the lightless air, my hand alights

to feel

if

you're

still there.

And you're still there. . .

IN THE SHOWER

facing you
I feel
as I
once did
years ago
before
the mirror,
dressing up,
believing
I could be
anyone.

Someday
we may
learn to forget
the distinctions
between
tears and other
forms of water,
why the halo

is not meant
to hover
above us
but to
pierce
the body
like a discus:
rapid, gold
light and
spinning.

PETITE MORT

I stand behind her breathing warmly upon her neck
undoing the faux pearl buttons on her charcoal dress.

Two hours ago she buried her mother. Gladiolas
and irises nonchalantly tossed upon the hardwood casket.

She said, "Do whatever you wish, but don't say a word until I'm fin-
ished." I press her down onto her knees

as if guiding her in prayer. She reminds me her mother was an atheist
and when the tumor in her brain

had swelled to the size of a small balloon, she'd say disturbing things like,
"What else is left for me but the shovel

and the worm." Two fingers inside her, circling as she drips
like rain from the wing of a gravestone angel. I know her

pastor couldn't comfort her like this—flashes of heaven, firing neu-
rons, the surging blood. The oblong hole, she

described as strewn with bits of mangled roots and tear- shaped
stones. "I watched the earth ingest her casket."

In twenty minutes, she insists her pleasure has diminished,
then calmly says, "You should really go." As I dress,

I stealthily glance at her. She rocks herself slowly, in cadence like a mother-
less crib, a boat released in twilight, left adrift.

CHAPEL

Laundry strung between high windows, billowy
in breezy light. A circle of uniformed boys

in a courtyard kicking a soccer ball, and someone
upstairs practicing piano. In the dream

a ceramic creamer painted with wild sunflowers.
Streaks of rainbow plumage from small boats

going away. Motor oil. Olive oil. Angels that leap
from the mind onto the chapel ceiling, a man supine

in midair—this is renovation. Now we must wait
for the fish light to surface: a mackerel or a perch.

Rust-colored sausages in a butcher shop dangling
like wind chimes. When I woke, the actual creamer

was bursting with purple grapes, the soccer ball beneath
the staircase, unnoticed, like the world. We say

we have come to gather the bright scales of desire,
though the early fog has swallowed canals and the sea.

It's barely dawn. We should sleep. Somewhere a painter
dips her brush, adding pale blue to the wings.

ON THE NIGHT SHE LEAVES ME WITH
THE JEWELS OF OUR SLEEPLESSNESS

Sanitation trucks at 4:00 AM grind north along Eighth Avenue
                                        mimicking the clatter
of an agitated solitude.

Her body asleep beside my body.
                        The arch of her a night-warm sheltering.

        The anagram of *need* is *Eden*.
                                Her absence carves a casket out of air.

        I wanted her mouth always,
                                even when pungent with chili paste and kimchi.

Only hours ago, I watched each tear

                drop

            from its

                eyelash
                        like crystals from a trembling chandelier.

PHOENIX

It was the wrong time and place
to look for resurrection.
Memorial Day, ninety-nine Fahrenheit, cloudless
sky, congested boulevards,
no parking spaces at the mall. Blinding sunlight
and the world on sale.
Always more loss required, always.
And after, feeble gestures to shape
what remains into a marvelous bird.

It would have been fine with me
to know only enough of grief
to raise a wren or sparrow. A tiny
passing song from a little mound
of soot. No, no, says your heart,
make a peregrine falcon, a red-tailed
hawk. Hoard loss until you hear
the last sweep of its wings.

I was told go to this city where
firebirds rush through the air
of burnt light, where imported palm
trees tilt and slump above the sand.
What rises is not a bird or the soul
offered relief, but scents of fast
food burger grease, cod and pollack
frying at Long John Silvers.

It's not your fault your name intimates
magic. To walk these streets
is to walk on coals. I was without her.
I needed someplace to take my ashes.

MINOTAUR

Was she disgusted by the coarseness of my beard, the toenails
I forgot to clip, or thoroughly repulsed by the pus-red

splotch between my ribs—an old wound from a picador?
Since she seldom spoke, all I could hear was her audible body

wanting to be sated: Do unto me. I am the day lily, and you— the towering
shadow that leads away. Whatever she sought

I can't quite imagine: the ardent grunt, the ravenous horn
perpetually erect. I admit it troubled me when she insisted:

"I only want to fuck you with the lights out." I bristled as any mortal would, feeling
hideous and vile, sensing her struggle to

save herself from me. The self in tiny duplicates in the mirrors
of her irides. The room completely dark. The thread that tied us

to the flaming center reeled back in and severed. An empty space
beside me. She's left the bed to dress. Elastic sounds of bra

and panties, her slowly fading scent. Blue jeans then a T-shirt slipped over
head, water jetting in the bathroom sink, her wish

that both of us would vanish. My sallow bull eyes follow
as she goes. The tiny crimson beacon of her burning cigarette.

THE AFFAIR

I want what I want when I want it.

This is not a song. It is an oak split
by lightning. Charcoal cankering
the wood's core. Chain saws arriving
after, and maybe a friend suggesting

I build a feeder for crows and mourning
doves. The direction of fire is
not for us to know. The wind pushes
wind into the middle of a living room,
or north where snow is falling.

I see Prometheus erotically now.
His bed of warm sand. Tied there.
The cold authority of the sun. Harpies
dressed in evening wear, vicious teeth.

STATUE OF EROS WITHOUT WINGS

I think there was no joy
in what was fought for.
Welts where the wings were.
A few feathers of a hen
after the fox has run.
What of the wholeness his body
wanted to belong to? Bone-yellow
hunk of torso bolted to a pedestal.
The radiance used up.
Only his heart lost within stone,
working like wings: that pitiful
flapping as he plummets.

DOGWOOD TIME

I wanted nothing
but to sit, and to breathe within
this white asylum,

cloistered as a sky-
blue Mary.
I'm certain if I hadn't

been at risk of arrest
for loitering, I would
have sat interminably

on the sidewalk on Perry Street,
trying to relinquish
the surges of self-pity.

But soon must come the nails and
blood and city policemen

incorrigible,
with nightsticks and flip pads
to write summonses.

ARCHAEOLOGY OF WATER

Ashley left during the last cold days of winter.
The winds were penniless
and the branches pressed against the sky like scars engraved on a living body.

Time refused its ordinary passage.
The hours fallow without measure.
Each day boxed in on the office calendar like rooms without windows.

I was ashamed of being left, having loved, having
been, it seemed, I thought, loved too, then left.

No films, no books, no music.
Only falsehoods unearthed in words.

And a last recourse: to perform an archaeology of water,
alone at the winter river north of Chelsea Piers,
before the stunning moon goes rotten.

Because I cannot extricate the gift from the wound,
I must wait for the moon to open its sarcophagi
and allow me to touch the shining pieces of what was.

SWANS, PENGUINS, WHALES & US
after Masaccio's *The Expulsion from the Garden of Eden*

On the body of the blue whale many colonies
of barnacles thriving. Swans coiffure their wings
numerous times per day to keep their feathers
perfectly white. And penguins pass their lives
on icebergs that glow like massive diamonds
in sunlight. This is all I know
of those creatures that mate for life.

When I lived with Laura,
I saw a gradual change come over her body:
her skin becoming mirror, then myself
deranged as in a cubist painting. One eye
on my cheekbone. One eye on my forehead.
Ear on my shoulder like an awkward wing.

The rest was long silences, reaching for
the butter instead of having it passed,
sitting on opposite ends of the sofa watching
Wild Kingdom and Jacques Cousteau explain
how other creatures shielded each other
from predators, adapting once the water
receded and earth was a place we could return to.

Months of strain caused the mirror to flake,
chip, and fall away and I gazed rapaciously
at the skin I loved to stroke, to slip into
my mouth, that she would not let me touch. There were
nights while she snored gently,
I lay beside her staring at the ceiling fan.
The wooden blades cutting apart the nothingness.

How once inside Santa Maria del Carmine
we gazed upon them as they stepped beyond
the Garden, not knowing where to go, shameful
in the light that could not cleanse them. I wondered
to myself, How will they help each other now?
Her hands covering her genitals and breasts.
His hands pressed trembling on his penitent eyes.

FLORENTINE SUNLIGHT

The odors were a mixture that lingered on my calfskin coat:
olives, polenta, hints of musty catacombs, fava beans and grappa. Men from
Ghana set their wares along the Ponte Vecchio:
antelopes, giraffes, and tribal figurines, the goddesses who uphold
heaven. I paused to watch the Arno flow its slightly grimy
malachite beyond the final city bridge, deciding not to pose for
a quick charcoal sketch, for who really needs to see oneself again,
living a second, insentient life as a portrait hung above the bed.

At JFK, I noticed others taking them with care through Customs:
scrolled on beige newsprint, frayed along the edges. Forms
reborn in profane ash, no angel's wings clasped to their backs,
no eye gleam of amazement, no heart gaze of compassion.
It was hell enough to walk among the fountains: all the chiseled
heroes with gull-white scrota. These grim reflections passing
crowded shops – I could never conquer wanting to be loved.

Scarves of silk, pocketbooks and upscale gloves, pastel shadows
varnishing the air, where I glimpsed her in an ancient courtyard:
A girl adorned in primrose crown who stands alone forever. I didn't
stop to consider what desire imagines. What was she but a heart-
beat
a stone god can't remember, garlic in the wind, fresh leather.

NOT KNOWING WHAT WILL HEAL HIM

Synagogue, psychotherapy, backpacking, zazen,
an entire shelf of self-help books all underlined
and dog-eared. He's tried just about everything
to cope, but within the moment of mirrored light
it was like trying to plug Old Faithful with his thumb.

He admits he is driven to go under the skin,
below id, within eternal light where the soul
is supposed to root tall and supple as an iris.
But what did he ever find beneath the flesh?
Monologues of the lonely body, Bardo, brief song.

He remembers his high school biology lab:
the frog's rubbery musculature, the purplish
calf's heart laid on newsprint, a gelatinous mass
vile and sad on the sterile altar in between
the Bunsen burners. He's never learned to linger

sufficiently in misery with his own mind
or any other to know if there are undiscovered
orchards beyond the crow-swarmed landfill.
Although he lights candles and smells the winter
pines, without her, he is frog skin, empty.

IV

BORDERS AND CROSSINGS

Everywhere I go I find a poet has been there before me.
—Sigmund Freud

BACKSEAT

This is not a joy ride, the upholstery
where I lost my virginity, or the open window
where I hung out my head to vomit tequila.

Her ex-lover has won her back. The wind
constant in my eyes. We pass a mongrel
abandoned along the highway. Everywhere

a fine for littering. Their voices after lust,
weary yet elated. They take turns driving.
They want to trust each other. I don't ask

to sit behind the wheel. On the highway
it is natural to speak of a future. She glances
in the mirror to check if I'm still there, to say

she needs some distance to clarify things, the way
astronauts try to comprehend the earth by gazing
back on it. They share a sixty-four ounce Coke:

A Big Boy. You're a big boy, aren't you? Well then,
stop whimpering. You've had enough candy.
Endless tar straightaway through saguaro, ocotillo.

There's supposed to be an oasis with slot machines
and cheap prime rib where I'd gladly hop out.
Sometimes the music on the radio is good, maybe

only because it is familiar. She claims she doesn't
sing, though once, pressed into me
I heard her hum softly. The fool steps to the edge

of the cliff admiring a broken daisy. So what
if I'm just going for a ride, I can doze
and greet the wind. I have the backseat to myself.

GALLUP

Along the pocked road snaking scrub
hills into Zuni Pueblo, two dead
mongrels and the windblown hollow
cartons of Budweiser twelve-packs.
Winter on old Route 66, twenty men
loiter outside the Hotel Lexington.
Men with nowhere to go, but away:
beyond the rusted boxcars, pawnshops,
the just-for-tourist tepees.

*

A gusty summer evening in Gallup,
free in the saddle, unencumbered,
quarters for Los Lobos and Patsy Cline.
Warm tortilla like a magician's handkerchief
covers my hands. Make her appear
so we can reminisce over shots of Cuervo.
In the unlit window one kachina
grips a bolt of lightning, one waves
a cornstalk in a song for the rain.
I wish the waitress would turn the lights
low and hold me till the flush of dawn
in a slow hip-to-hip country swing.

*

I didn't buy a concha belt from the staggering
Navajo headed for Lukachukai, nor offer
a ride to his loop-legged friends perched
on milk crates beside the package store.
To know what the drum knows, the eaglet
chained to the ancient roof, new shoot
of a bean sprout risen in fragile triumph.
Where to root? Where are the chains of home?
Just this drum, unaccompanied heart,
days remote from everyone I care for.

*

Pulling out of Motel 6 at daybreak,
pale faced, hung over, in terra-cotta
light. Towers of sandstone, ticking
dust. Which map will guide the tumble-
weed migrating nowhere? A piece
of conversation overheard by the pumps
at Thriftway: Those Navajos got money
for liquor and nothing else.
Two hundred miles from Flagstaff,
scalding coffee, a powwow of ghosts,
the warm, whorled body of a sweet roll.

*

All morning straight-lined on Interstate 40,
unsure which is destination, which is detour.

The azure-filled socket of Window Rock off 264.
The skyward ladders surging up from Second Mesa.

If only justice was a satisfied coyote who stood
completely still, and wouldn't slither away again

like luck, love, money.

*

AT THE PAIR-A-DICE BAR

Half the men in Paradise, Montana
are missing limbs.

Their burly forms perched on barstools,
tranquilized by dismantling,

gripping chilled Coors
in the nimble vices

of their claws. One old fellow sings
with Merle Haggard

about scoundrels and outlaws,
while I muse in a rust-red booth,

remembering the sketchbooks of Durer
and Leonardo: a foot, a pure

hand, a luminous torso. The beauty
of all that is partial.

CANVAS AND DISTANCE

Outside Bozeman we stopped for cigarettes. She spoke of
what was worth suffering for. Only love and art, truth
and song. Wired on No-Doz, we checked-in, in the middle
of nowhere. 3:00 AM, HBO, complimentary doughnuts at sunrise.
Our room reeking of dead cigars and tropical cologne.

Abbott and Costello on cable TV, then Fred with Ginger
whirling in their elegant helix. She chain-smoked, quoted
Baudelaire, though her icons didn't seem to help her.

Balthus painted felines with human souls. Bacon
painted slabs of beef with a rotten, cosmic glow.
Two partly devoured shapes blasted by cacophonous A/C,
cooling down atop the bedspread, inhaling their sexual decay.
Some frames we were never meant to inhabit.

*

Driving from Big Sky to Enchantment. All those pretty license plates
stamped out in penitentiaries. Mindlessly calm in the dawn light
east of Abiquiu, where I pulled over, wide-eyed, between beige spires.

Umber dripping russet from inner stillness. At sea in the dryness,
under fish clouds, under bone clouds, ignited by the sandstone flames.

*

Days after dropping her off in Taos I stood in a thrift shop
in the town where the bomb was invented. A long rack

of wedding gowns on sale near the back: spangled, glittering
like freshly gessoed canvas. How odd, this urge to try one on

and stand before the mirror in drag. The bride of Los Alamos
without a vow to anyone, followed by cow skulls and gorgons

of toxic clouds into a sunbaked plaza in Jemez where children
danced resplendent in plumage: kestrel, eagle, red-tailed hawk.

FERMENTATION

In the Old World, the workers took
their shoes off to press the Pinot Noir.

There is sadness in arriving before the harvest,
and a bitter taste. The sacrament

of feet stained the color of fresh blood
above me in the cool, white Mission.

The purpose of the grape—crush the flesh
into the spirit, the spirit into endless

longing. Napa, Saint. Helena, Calistoga,
early grapes in taut dark clusters.

Migrant workers on their knees
watched by tourists on the Wine Train.

To merely stroll the vineyard paths
keeps us from the underworld,

at least for now. The train ride is nearly
over, and yet, always, this other life:

where we sink among ripened grapes,
vanish into the skins of broken fruit.

WATER AND THE GLASS THAT CONTAINS IT

"I am only other when I am myself, my acts are more my own when they are everybody because to be myself I must be other, go out of myself, seek my self among others." —Octavio Paz

ABOUT THE HOURS

For twenty miles of dirt road, we followed the sugarcane tractors.
Wilted cornstalks in April heat. A young mother with a pail on one arm
and a newborn in the other. Blackened fields in the distance billowing
bluish smoke. The tour bus pulled up to a dingy cantina. Rhythm
of a woman's hands stacking fresh tortillas. Sun-drained, parched,
a slowness had entered us, and it didn't matter anymore
about the hours.

TIN BELLS

Outside the sugar factory a schoolboy guides a rusted bicycle
by the handlebars past four slim, mustachioed men

walking with machetes at their hips. On the bus
I overhear one American say to another, There

are no signs here. How does anyone find their way.
Noontime carries echoes of bells and the shadows of insects

circumscribed by silence. Sunlight in the eyes
of two stone horses, each with a headless rider.

LOS ANGELITOS

The infant coffins on display in Catemaco
are empty, thank God.
But you must know, my friend, that children die here.
Limes, red chilies, oranges and corn, the river
and the well, her eyes
and the clover honey gathered there.

On a brittle wall the faded words: LAS MANOS
DE LA RESURRECCIÓN. The task,

the casket dealer told me, is to live as if
already in the afterlife.

Little coffin, little tomb boat,
even without wind or water, each of us is ferried away.

MEXICAN CEMETERY

I came upon white towers in the city of the dead:
wreaths, lavish bows and tattered lace, red plastic roses
overturned among the weeds, ponderous headstones
of cement cooling in the banyans' shadows. A child's pink
church dress drying by itself on a clothesline.

LITTLE PRAYER

Virgin of the weeping corn,
Madonna of the buried newborn,

Take me
famished as I am

to your turquoise breast,
to your bleeding doves.

SNAPSHOT

Procession of sluggish donkeys, saddlebags loaded with corn.
Rice seed and black wands of sugarcane scattered
on the roads.
Again, the dust—inhaled, tasted, settled on the wide mosaic of pores.
Mud walls crumbling and fallen. Townsfolk
coming and going

from the market before dark with tamarind candies and dolls of felt
and straw. Factory workers, friends and strangers,

young lovers, and a busload

of gringos hoping for the perfect snapshot. . . Soon the merchants
will pack up and depart with their burlap sacks
of garlic and peanuts,

leaving the plaza empty. For the moment though, it's impossible
to forget the sound of one's own vanishing.
A lantern blown out before sleep.

SUGAR SMOKE

Beyond Los Mangos, warm breezes fragrant with burnt
sugarcane, the russet of drought. Onion vendors lining

the market road. Gold and purple onions, their skins white
as parchment, as the Anglo body. Her spare and simple room:

two plastic chairs, a kettle and a table, a cot and a calendar
with a painting of the resurrection tacked to the wall.

Her hair, unpinned, torrential, darker than frijoles. And like
the sea, the sound of her hairbrush, over and over and over.

VESSEL WITH PAINTED AZTEC WARRIORS

Empty me
that I may be

simply

eyes that gaze upon the work
of love.

THE ACCORDION PLAYERS

The poor accordion players of Oaxaca stand on narrow sidewalks
near the plaza, alongside a yellow wall, beside another wall painted
eggshell blue. Stoic in the dry heat, solemn in their scuffed
black shoes.
                        Tortillas made fresh on the griddle only cost a few centavos
and the loveliness of their offered song is free, though the blind
man has already paid dearly with his eyesight and his nine-year-old son
with truancy from the local elementary school.
                                        The music hums as vendors
pass with whirligig toys, plastic kites and silver bracelets, a rainbow
panoply
of helium balloons. The musician's daughter in a frilly white
dress serenely
holds a red plastic donation bowl and waits for every song to finish.
                                                        She follows
anxiously behind me pleading for more pesos. *"Senor, senor, por
favor me madre muerte."* But I hurry fast away, away from a child's
talk of death over the sun-gold cobblestones.

                                        At the edge of the city, I come
upon a simple graveyard. Pastel-colored angels shaded by lethargic
willows.
Is her mother buried here, I wonder. Has anyone left for her a
single artificial rose?
                        I return to the zocalo at dusk. Another boy is playing
solo. Accordion on his lap, heavier than his own small torso. "Donde
esta tu padre," I ask, after dropping a few coins in his dish.
But he doesn't answer, doesn't lift his gaze to acknowledge
that I've spoken.
                        He taps the buttons rapidly, fills the old machine
with air. Empties it and fills it, droning on and on with a grave,
ferocious sorrow. *Is your father home asleep? Resting in a nearby bar
easing his weariness with friends and cold cerveza?*
                                        Although I've shut
my hotel window from the midnight sounds of the plaza, their music
seeps inside me. Son and father playing on through the night,
pressing down hard on the white keys of my bones.

235

TASCO TRIPTYCH

I. *Maundy Thursday*

All night I have listened to the rap of metal
chains across old cobblestones, and not forgiven
anyone and not forgiven myself. How dark

must it become? Darker than a bloodstain,
darker than a horse. Death alone and no one
come to comfort the poor clay of his body.

All night the red-mouthed gladiola burn
beside the honey tapers, and the thorns that he wore
are the thorns in which we kneel, then lie down.

II. *Holy Hour*

Propped up in bed beside the scripture of your sleep
I listen to the dogs of moonlit indigo scavenge the trash-
heaped hills. Radiance brocaded on the convoluted sheet
and the flesh spun about your neck equal to the shadow
of a lily. Somnolent dogs in the empty pews outstretched
beneath his spike-pierced feet. Dawn contained within
amethyst walls. On the shores of prayer, I see no one.

III. *Madrugada*

Follow the milk-wax drippings over the silver-gray stones.
The whole moon is a newly minted peso watched
by insidious guard dogs. A mask maker sleeps below

the skeletal faces, while his seamstress wife hurries
to finish the last of the penitents' hoods. It is required
that you grieve alone like Jesus among Roman soldiers,

to suffer with your back turned to the
world. With prayer and nothing else, daybreak belongs
to God only and the shadows of passing birds.

236

DARK SQUARE

We will all die dreaming something of this world:

its eggs, dust, feathers,
and its body of bread.

            On moonless nights
the whole house
sways with sleep.

      At dawn, a marlin arcs and wavers
toward the Mexican sun.

Murmuring children pass
through the graveyard gates, carrying little pines.

AFTER VALLEJO
"Every bone in me belongs to others; and maybe I robbed them. I came to
take something for myself that maybe was meant for some other man."
—Caesar Vallejo

Each morning in Lima near the sea,
instruction or observation:

Beneath the stone head of the condor
gather the windblown petals.

      *

Each afternoon the scrawny boys waited nearby
as I sipped iced coffee,

                      then hurried alongside me across the plaza,
desperate to shine my rubber sandals.

      *

The giant bells of Jesus overhead.
The little bells of push-cart men selling
ice cream cones and fresh-pressed orange juice.

The whisperings of school girls and lovers and those
in the silence of exile, standing by themselves,
their backs pressed to sunlit walls as if before an execution.

      *

Disheveled beggars linger below an urban cross
as if waiting there to witness to the actual crucifixion.

I purchase one ripe, unblemished mango from a somnolent vendor.
An offering to no one.

It is heavy in my hands
like something stolen.

      *

What was left of the market at twilight:

A smashed banana, the brittle hairs of coconut husks,
a few scattered kernels of corn.

One gray mule tethered to a rickety cart.
Within one umber dome of an eye: the watery shadow I always was.

*

Then the rain fell lightly, lighter than the coins in my trouser pocket.
I can't remember when it was I began to turn from other's despair.

It is raining and I remember
the cruel caverns of my ingratitude.

*

I couldn't discern if it was hope or instruction:
you will write about their shoes

and those without shoes
and those with torn and muddied feet

and those without feet and the man sliced right in half
at the hips who totters on the palms of his hands.

*

                    At the door of the lion
the loneliness was not worse.

Saffron paint formed an oblong
                    of daylight and on

the next street a man
                    who insisted,

                                        you must keep walking
until you see
the horse who carries angels.

                              Instead, I met a pauper leaning on a wooden

crutch
begging beside a stagnant fountain.
His left leg amputated

just below the knee.
Stallion of a man

mid-gallop

*

The earth holds the edges of a coffin in its darkness.

Amigo, please teach me

how to cling

to the tin rim   of her halo.

*

One man played accordion by the sea.
Another opened a spout in a coconut

pouring its clear milk into a cone-
shaped paper cup.

White geraniums.
Fallen mangos.

Lime and cilantro as I slept
and when I woke.

Santo Domingo alone on the shore,
indolent, stoic

as the bobbing heads slid under.
I should have gone down, I should

have gone down
on my knees with the others.

*

I met Blanca on a crowded bus and she brought me
to her home. She handed me the tepid chicha, then pointed

where the sunlight fell in the unkempt garden. The red
and green Christmas lights of ripening jalapenos, the dwarf

pillars of corn. I played futbol with her nephews, admired
a tattered doll shared by two sisters, though its button-eyes

were missing and left with hanging threads for vision.
With a tin platter placed before me at the table,

the children serenaded a high, soprano grace.
A boiled chicken clawing the air slaughtered in my honor.

*

In darkness, a glow recurrent in the rooms of lovers.
Golden light on the empty balconies.

Each cobblestone containing a private loneliness.
Each cobblestone set in the earth—a fragment of someone's future grave.

Men leaning on walls. Men receding
into corners, reading what remains of other people's news,

listening to what remains of other people's songs,
waiting for the moment to put out our darkness with our shadow.

*

The bus crept torpidly along rutted roads towards Urcos.
In the end you will arrive where you are supposed to arrive.

A ghostly cry appeased at the breast.
Those who slept with open mouths as if they were singing.

NOTES:

From Everything A Little Remains: Bonfim ribbons are worn as symbols of faith and for seeking of various blessings within the Bahia faith that predominates in Salvador, Brazil.

Last Call: The bodran is a traditional Irish hand-held drum.

Belonging: La Repubblica is the major daily newspaper published in Rome.

Above Debed Canyon: Nostrovia is the quintessential word used in making toasts, meaning "cheers" and/or "to your health."

The City of Rivers and Angels & **Sand then Mirror then the Given Light**: Nevsky Prospekt is a shopping/nightlife thoroughfare in St. Petersburg, Russia.

A Short History of Flight: The italicized passages are quotations from an array of famous flyers including: The Wright Bros., Amelia Earhart, Charles Lindberg, The Birdman of Alcatraz, the Apollo 11 astronauts and historians or journalists who r ecounted their biographical exploits.

Two Markets: Uzbekistan: Som is the name of the currency in Uzbekistan.

Gravel Children's Song: Puja used by both Hindus and Buddhists in India and the region to denote acts of prayer, worship and devotion.

The River and the Wheel: A ghat in India is a series of steps that leads to the banks of a sacred body of water, most often a holy river.

Need Heaven: Jama Masjid is the main and largest mosque in Delhi.

The Mingun Bell: Kyat is the name of the currency in Myanmar.

S-21: the code name for Tuol Sleng, a former school converted by the Khmer Rouge into a center for interrogation and torture, which inevitably led to death. Kkoy Tiel is a popular and traditional Cambodian soup akin to Vietnamese pho.

The Pornography of Napalm: is based on the horrific war photograph taken by Nick Ut of napalmed children running for their lives from the village of Trang Ban in 1972.

Luoi: Luoi translated from the Vietnamese means "tongue."

Basho and Togoe after the Little Boy: Little Boy was the code name for the atomic bomb dropped on Hiroshima. The last line comes from Basho.

Travelers of the Dreamless Hours: Ginebras is the brand name of cheapest gin found ubiquitously throughout the Philippines.

Jet Lag in Fragments: Kamben is traditional Balinese attire, identical to the Indian sarong.